Burst
Believers II

by Vic DaPra

FIRST EDITION

ISBN: 978-1-57424-310-9

SAN 683-8022

Cover and layout by James Creative Group

Copyright © 2014 CENTERSTREAM Publishing LLC
P.O. Box 17878 – Anaheim Hills, CA 92817 www.Centerstream-USA.com

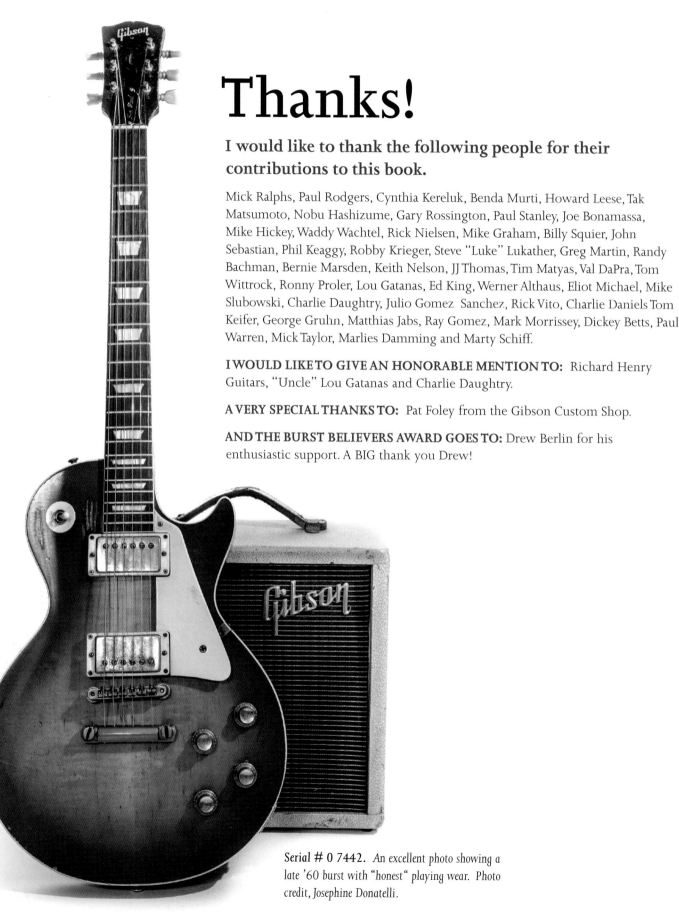

Thanks!

I would like to thank the following people for their contributions to this book.

Mick Ralphs, Paul Rodgers, Cynthia Kereluk, Benda Murti, Howard Leese, Tak Matsumoto, Nobu Hashizume, Gary Rossington, Paul Stanley, Joe Bonamassa, Mike Hickey, Waddy Wachtel, Rick Nielsen, Mike Graham, Billy Squier, John Sebastian, Phil Keaggy, Robby Krieger, Steve "Luke" Lukather, Greg Martin, Randy Bachman, Bernie Marsden, Keith Nelson, JJ Thomas, Tim Matyas, Val DaPra, Tom Wittrock, Ronny Proler, Lou Gatanas, Ed King, Werner Althaus, Eliot Michael, Mike Slubowski, Charlie Daughtry, Julio Gomez Sanchez, Rick Vito, Charlie Daniels Tom Keifer, George Gruhn, Matthias Jabs, Ray Gomez, Mark Morrissey, Dickey Betts, Paul Warren, Mick Taylor, Marlies Damming and Marty Schiff.

I WOULD LIKE TO GIVE AN HONORABLE MENTION TO: Richard Henry Guitars, "Uncle" Lou Gatanas and Charlie Daughtry.

A VERY SPECIAL THANKS TO: Pat Foley from the Gibson Custom Shop.

AND THE BURST BELIEVERS AWARD GOES TO: Drew Berlin for his enthusiastic support. A BIG thank you Drew!

Serial # 0 7442. An excellent photo showing a late '60 burst with "honest" playing wear. Photo credit, Josephine Donatelli.

Burst
Believers II

Serial # 9 2072.

John Sebastian

I first encountered my favorite Les Paul in a small club in Greenwich Village. Skip Boone, brother to Spoonful bassist Steve Boone, in a band pointedly named the Sellouts, played it. This was a time of relentlessly acoustic and traditional music in the village.

Skip and his band were pushing hard at that envelope, playing rockabilly, Beatles covers, and generally raising the rafters. The Spoonful, at that time was still forming, but I was already in search for a guitar that would do the unthinkable in downtown circles. Finger picking on an electric guitar! Oh yeah, and could it have a Gibsony radius? Skips' guitar had it all. I was in the midst of trying everything at Mannys' music, and I could tell there wasn't anything like it there.

On the chances I got to play the instrument in between sets, I could tell it was beefy. Remember, very few people (myself included) understood the distinction between single coil and humbucking pick-ups, or what a maple cap does. I only knew that this guitar could fill up enormous amounts of bottom end, perfect to contrast the ice pick-to-the-brain treble of Zal Yanovskys' Guild Thunderbird.

Within weeks, Skip began to yearn for a newer stereo Gibson (remember, with your choice of 6 lousy

Photo credit, Dion Ogust

6

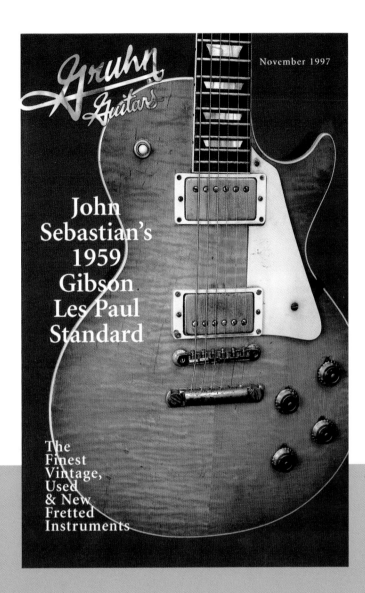

John
Sebastian's
1959
Gibson
Les Paul
Standard

The
Finest
Vintage,
Used
& New
Fretted
Instruments

November 1997

sounds?) and asked if I'd be interested in the guitar. I tried to conceal my glee, even though it was expensive (wait for it...) $125 dollars.

The instrument went right to work. It ended up on ALL Spoonful recordings with medium gauge flat-wound 57-13 strings, always providing a suitably corpulent bottom end for autoharps, acoustics, Marxophones, and Zal Yanovskys' genius guitar playing. And I wasn't always playing it. In the days before Anvil cases and multiple roadies, the Spoonful operated with very few guitars, so when we needed another overdub, we'd switch guitars, knowing our instruments sounded completely different when we switched.

By this time, Zal and Michael Bloomfield had become fast friends. At some point I pulled out the instrument. "OH MY GOD what is that? Bloomfield was always explosive. "Man, that is just so much cooler than the gold. I gotta have one!". Within weeks he had topped my modest plaintop with a lovely flamey caramel colored burst that became his most visible guitar.

The instrument continued to serve me through a whole second career of out door venues (post Woodstock) and on into the early nineties, when I took it off the road because of its' provenance, and began to use a Heritage archtop in its' place.

— John Sebastian

Probably the first rock record sleeve to feature a burst. The English invasion begins and the burst makes its way into rock history.

Serial # 9 0291. *An original owner burst from North Carolina with an intensely flamed top and a strong vivid sunburst finish...One of the best!*

Mick Taylor

In 1967 I was playing guitar for John Mayall's Bluesbreakers and I was told by Ian Stewart that Keith was selling his Les Paul, the one that he used on Satisfaction.

I wanted it, so I went to Olympic Studios in Barnes and was shown the guitar in a small room off the main studio. I bought it there and then at the asking price.

After I got the guitar, I went into the main studio where the Stones were working on 'Satanic Majesties', dressed in psychedelic costumes. That's the only time I ever saw Brian Jones.

In June 1969 I joined the Rolling Stones. This Les Paul 1959 Sunburst with bigsby was my favourite guitar. I never asked Keith why he had decided to sell it.

The guitar got stolen in the infamous raid on Nellcôte in the south of France when we were recording Exile and I never saw it again.

If anyone has information on the guitar's whereabouts, please e-mail: micktaylor@post.com

Photo credit, Dominique Tarlé.

Serial # 9 0627

Paul Rodgers

When Free toured with Blind Faith in 1969 Koss swapped his guitar with Clapton at the end of the tour. I bought it some years after Paul's death, mostly for sentimental reasons. It is a wonderful, powerful instrument. I wrote some songs with it including Satisfaction Guaranteed which I recorded with Jimmy Page in The Firm. I took the guitar on tour in '85 and Syd, my guitar tech at the time slept with it in his hotel room every night to keep it safe!!

Given the time Koss acquired the guitar and the time we recorded All Right Now, released in May 1970 I'm pretty sure it is the guitar that he played when we recorded All Right Now.

Thanks to the current owner John Oxman for bringing the guitar to Woodstock, N.Y., July 27, 2013 and allowing it to be played that night and for his kind open offer to for me to play it anytime in the future."

— Paul Rodgers

Is the Missing Cream Burst Really Missing?

My love affair with Bursts began in 1964, when I saw The Rolling Stones on the Ed Sullivan show. Keith was playing a really cool Burst with a Bigsby. I knew it was a Gibson Les Paul, but I didn't know the model. Even though the show was in black and white, I still got the full impact of how cool it looked and sounded. I knew I had to have one. In July 1966, it was an electric guitar player's duty to buy John Mayall's album Blues Breakers With Eric Clapton, and learn every lick on that record. Blues Breakers was the starting point for the definitive Rock sound: The American craftsmanship of a Gibson, through the British perfection that was a Marshall amp.

Serial # 9 2024. Photo credit, Patrick Stevenson

Whether or not you consider Eric Clapton the main influence of the British Blues Invasion, you can't deny the huge role he played in moving the sound forward. In that same vein, you also can't deny that the Burst helped increase the impact of this new, invincible sound. With his first Burst resonating throughout Blues Breakers, and his second Burst blazing through uncharted territory on Fresh Cream, you would think that it would be impossible for these guitars to disappear from the limelight. This wasn't the case. We've all heard the story that the Beano Burst was stolen, that's the legend. As for the second guitar, the Fresh Cream Burst, it was rumored that it went missing, or that it was broken. With no definitive answer, the question remains: What happened to the second Clapton Burst? Well, I am qualified to answer that question. I currently have the guitar in my possession, and being a trusted member of the Burst community, I can assure you that yes: it is definitely the Fresh Cream Burst.

Since the Burst Believers book came out, I have had the pleasure of connecting several first time burst buyers with their dream guitar. I love watching the magic of these guitars instantly turn into inspiration for their new owner. I'm glad that Vic is out there with his passion and commitment for the burst to make sure it gets the recognition it deserves. There is no other guitar as illusive as the burst, and it's thanks to Vic that they've continued to remain in the spotlight for all generations of players.

In 1966, after the Beano Burst was stolen, Clapton called up Andy Summers, who had originally pointed him in the direction of the Beano Burst, and asked him to sell him his Burst. According to Andy Summers, in his biography, he sold the 1960 Burst to Eric for £200 and brought it to him at Advision in the West End, where he was recording with Jack Bruce and Ginger Baker. This particular guitar can be heard on most of the tracks on the Fresh Cream album, earning it the nickname the Fresh Cream Burst.

Eric, Jack and Ginger chose Cream as their name as they were the best players around at the time; the cream of the crop. Fresh Cream was this super group's introduction. Unleashing this sound, with Burst in hand, Clapton continued his reign as heavyweight champion of rock guitar. This may be the only Cream album where you can hear a Burst.

Okay, so it's clear that this Burst was used on Fresh Cream, but why was it not used again in the rest of Cream's short-lived career? In trying to understand these facts for myself, I traced the path this Burst took to New York City, 1967, where Eric and Cream were at the time. The road crew dropped the Fresh Cream Burst, and the headstock broke off. They then brought it to Dan Armstrong to have it repaired. He in turn, gave it to the best luthier in New York City, for whom no job was impossible. His name is Matt Umanov. Matt was very young when he discovered his talent for luthiery. The combination of his skills and talent were brought to the attention of world-class guitar players in need of the best sounding instruments. He quickly gained the reputation as the go-to guy in the New York area for restoration and repair of pre-war to current musical instruments. So Matt was clearly the guy to turn to in this situation.

So here's where the story gets interesting. When Dan Armstrong asked Matt to take up this challenge and repair the broken headstock, Matt realized at the time that the headstock could no longer be grafted back on to the guitar, due to the severity of the break. He then asked Dan if he could get creative with this project, to which Dan gave his approval. With Matt's history of passion and appreciation for pre-war Gibson mandolins, he thought it would be cool to replace the headstock with a Gibson F4 mandolin headstock. And so it was to be.

— **Drew Berlin**

Serial # 9 1923. *Nicknamed Donna.*

As a Burst collector who wanted flamey tops, I was always looking for something like the Brock Burst. When I got Donna 9-1923] I finally had it! Color and monster flame in great condition. Maybe too nice condition, as I have always been afraid to take it too far from home. I think this is the overall best Burst I have ever owned. Of course, I am very proud of that! At one time I got a chance to make some "baseball" type cards, and chose Donna as the subject.

— Tom Wittrock

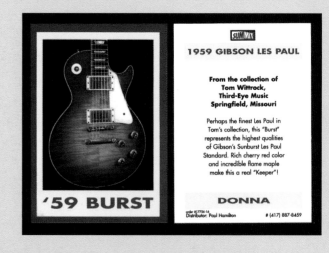

Ed King

Though I've made my living playing a Stratocaster, I always come back to original 58-60 Les Paul Models. Their tone gets all up inside my head to the point that's all I want to hear. The Gibson Custom Shop has released a series based on my '59. It's an insane guitar. The neck feel & fret job are PRECISE! To me, that's everything.

— Ed King

Serial # 9 1972.

A Collectors Dream

Here are a few pictures of the 1960 Burst. The serial number is # 0 0233. It was an early one with appointments of a 1959.

The story behind this guitar is a collectors dream story. This guitar was a birthday present for a very lucky 10 year old boy in Louisville, Ky. He told me that he played it for a couple of months and then put it in the case and didn't play it again. His Father said he could have any guitar in the store. There was a black Gibson Custom and this beautiful 1960 Burst. I think he made the right choice. When I went to look at the guitar and opened the case, I found that it still had the tissue paper wrapped around the guitar just as it did they day it left the store. I don't think I will ever find another one in this condition, but sure hope I do!

Jim Anderson assisted me with purchasing this guitar.

— **Daryl Marty Schiff**

Serial # 8 5386. Nicknamed "The Moonburst."

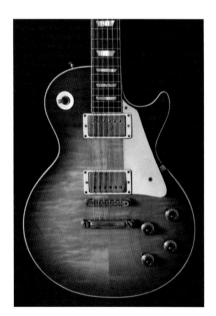

Serial # 9 0288. *An early 59 with original thin frets. The color is very similar to serial # 9 0291. Photo credit, Gruhn Guitars.*

Serial # 9 1921.

22

Serial # 0 0608. *An excellent example of an early '60 burst with strong color remaining, nicely bookmatced flamed maple top and a huge neck profile. Photo credit, Joe Menza.*

Serial # 9 1873

Dickey Betts

My first guitar I owned was a Stella archtop. In 1962 I played my first Gibson Les Paul. When I played with the Allmans I primarily played a Goldtop and a burst. I wasn't influenced by alot of the 'burst players at the time. I hope as time marches on, todays players will go back and listen to the early recordings and try to capture the tone we had. I am also proud to be part of the Gibson Custom Shop "Southern Rock Tribute Les Paul" this year.

— Dickey Betts

Serial # 9 1176. A nice moderately flamed '59 with all white coils in both chambers.

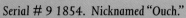

Serial # 9 1854. Nicknamed "Ouch."

Serial # 8 5521. This beauty was found by Gruhn Guitars in Nashville and is one of the most pristine bursts I've ever seen. The color looks like it did the day it left the factory. Photo credit, Charlie Daughtry.

Serial # 9 2024

Serial # 8 6900. One fine looking '58 burst and one fine photograph. Photo credit, Richard Henry Guitars.

29

Here's Johnny Depp picking out a '59 burst at Rumbleseat Music.

Serial # 9 2178. Johnny Depp's choice burst Nicknamed "Kramer."

Serial # 9 0637. *A very warm faded '59 with tight flame covering the top. Nicknamed "The Preacher."* Photo credit, Ricky Sanchez.

Serial # 9 0850. *Nicknamed 'The Believer Burst" by the Gibson Custom Shop.*

Serial # 9 1175.
An absolutely kick ass looking burst.

Serial # 9 0381. *A beautiful example of an "under the bed burst" that came up for sale recently.*
Photo credit, Artie Sonsini.

Serial # 0 0271. My 1960 Burst was the second Burst that I purchased. The dealer who sold me my 1959 Burst contacted me when he acquired this guitar, which came back from a collector in Japan, and after one look at the photos I had to have it! At one time in its history, this guitar was in Mac Yasuda's collection, and is pictured in his book, The Vintage Guitar Vol. 3 on page 51. It was a vibrant cherry sunburst at the time it was in Mac's collection, but prior to my acquiring it, the guitar had faded to a beautiful Teaburst color. You can still see some hints of red by the tone knobs and under the pickguard. This guitar is in near mint condition and plays and sounds great! None of my Bursts are flame monsters, but this one has the most figure of the three.

Serial # 9 1106. This burst came from the Preacher son of a Preacher who bought it from a traveler in the early '60s. The guitar was put away in '78 and it remained unplayed for 35 years. When 'discovered' it had 5 strings, white corrosion/funk all over the pickup rings, green frets, and a greenish fingerboard. 9 pounds, wonderful slim neck, and 2 double whites! Bill Fajen.

Serial # 9 1946. A stellar '59 with a gorgeous caramel faded sunburst. The butt end of the face shows traces of a once removed bigsby.

Serial # 9 2019

Serial # 9 0681. An absolutely stunning example of a '59 burst, great color and a perfect bookmatched maple top... nicknamed "Johnny". Photo credit, Charlie Daughtry.

Photo credit, Clay Patrick McBride

Gary Rossington

The first guitarist I really admired was Duane Allman. We grew up in Florida, fairly near each other so I got to hear him perform. I also loved the work and the sounds of Paul Kossoff, Jimmy Page, and Jeff Beck. But it was when I had the opportunity to play Charlie Daniels '59 Les Paul that I knew I had to have one.

Then one night we were playing at the " Briar Patch ", a club in Nashville. I started to talk to a girl and the conversation came around to old Les Paul's. She said she had an uncle, a cousin maybe, that had one. She drove me several miles into the country and pulled up to a farm house.

The guy inside went to a bedroom, reached under the bed and pulled the guitar out. I think I knew it was the real deal when I saw the case. Then he opened it... and there she was, a '59 Sunburst I would eventually call "Bernice".

All of the old songs and leads were written on her. The last time I saw her, she was at the Rock and Roll Hall Of Fame in Cleveland. She was in a double-cased display along side Duane's guitar.

It was a strange but wonderful "full circle of life moment".

— Gary Rossington

Serial # 9 0850. Another look at 'The Believer Burst."

Serial # 9 1152. Frank Pine's stunning '59 burst nicknamed "The Pine Burst."

Serial # 9 1061. Nicknamed "The Bahama Burst."

Serial # 0 7441. This burst was purchased in Frankfurt, Germany in 1978 and was formerly owned by Al Anderson from the Bob Marley Band. Photo credit, Andy Nowak.

Serial # 0 8600. Nicknamed "Shattered Glass", this burst displays a very "wild" looking top.

Serial # 9 1945. "Nicky."

Serial # 8 6893

Serial # 9 0696. This '59 was once owned by Gary Grainger of The Rod Stewart Band , hence the nickname "The Grainger."

Serial # 0 1500. Franco Tonini.

Serial # 9 0647

Serial # 9 1893. Very deep rich color over tight flames gives this burst a unique look.

A recent photo of Jeff at The Iridium in NYC playing a Les Paul Reissue at a Les Paul Tribute show.

Jeff Beck

In the days leading up to the Grammy Awards in Jan. 2010 I had a call from Jeff Beck's guitar tech Stevie Prior. Jeff was planning on playing "How High the Moon" as a tribute to Les Paul on the Grammy telecast. Gibson had recently created the Jeff Beck "Oxblood" Les Paul at the Custom Shop and Jeff brought along the prototype intending to use it on the Grammy performance. He thought it was a bit on the heavy side and asked if I had a couple of Custom Shop Les Pauls that he could try out. Custom Shop General Manager Rick Gembar asked me to gather up a few nice guitars and head out to LA. I had the pleasure of sitting with Jeff at the Sunset Marquis hotel while he tried out several re-issue Les Pauls. The one he decided on happened to be my own guitar. It is a heavily figured cherry sunburst 1958 reissue that was originally built for Mark Knopfler. Mark thought it was a bit too heavily flamed for his taste but I was in love with it, so I asked to buy it for myself. I

Serial # 9 1864. This photo is from the late 60s of "The Jeff Beck Group" with Jeff playing his 59 burst.

ended up modifying it slightly with the addition of wiring and pickups from the Jimmy Page #1. Jeff played it on the Grammys and asked if he could hold on to it for a while. He ended up playing the guitar at the Iridium shows with Imelda May on the 8th and 9th of June which became the "Rock n Roll Party" video honoring Les. I was fortunate to attend rehearsals and both nights of the show. As anyone who was at the Iridium or has seen the video will agree, only Jeff Beck could have pulled off recreating Les' songs on stage. He continued to play the guitar throughout the tour which followed. I finally connected with Jeff when he performed in Nashville later that year and managed to snag the guitar back. Besides owning a truly great Gibson Les Paul I also now am the proud owner of a small piece of Jeff Beck's legacy and I couldn't be more happy.

— Pat Foley

Serial # 0 7615. Photo credit, Rumbleseat Music.

Serial # 9 1953. The only burst I know of that has three nicknames "The Hawaiian ," "The Claw " and " Carmelita "... call it what you want but this is one outstanding burst.

Serial # 8 6784. An astounding '58 Les Paul Sunburst from the Charlie Daughtry collection. Nicknamed "Jennifer. "

Serial # 9 0592. Nicknamed "RJ."

George Gruhn

Gruhn Guitars Incorporated is essentially a hobby that got out of hand. I didn't buy my first guitar until I was a freshman in college at the University of Chicago. I started collecting insects when I was about four years old. By the time I was six years old I was collecting frogs and turtles and bringing them home as pets. I caught my first snake when I was eight years old. By the time I was 12 years old I was subscribing to the Journal of the American Society of Ichthyologists and Herpetologists. It was always assumed that I would grow up to be an academic zoologist. I have never taken any course in music or business. All of my academic background is in zoology and animal behavior psychology. At present I have about a dozen snakes and a lizard sharing my office with me.

I developed an interest in music and guitars during the folk music boom of 1959 through 1963 when I was a student at Oak Park River Forest High School in suburban Chicago. I have a brother 3 ½ years younger than me who started playing guitar before I did and many of my friends in high school and later in college when I went to the University of Chicago were very actively interested in traditional Appalachian string band music and bluegrass.

The University of Chicago Folklore Society as well as folklore societies at the University of Michigan in Ann Arbor, University of Illinois at Champaign Urbana, and the University Wisconsin in Madison and similar organizations in New York City area as well as in California were very active in sponsoring interest in old timey acoustic music and promoted concerts bringing back many of the performers who had been active as early as 1920s and 30s.

While I was interested in the music, I found that the guitars, mandolins, and banjos I saw being used fascinated me fully as much if not more than the music itself. Before I ever learn to play a note on a guitar I was very familiar with many Martin and Gibson models. My parents were willing to fund the purchase of one good guitar for me, but I soon discovered that I had an addiction for collecting fretted instruments specimens much as I had been doing with reptiles since childhood. I quickly discovered that in my searches of music stores, pawn shops, classified newspaper ads that for every instrument I unearthed which was of interest to me for my personal collection, I would uncover 50 or more that were great deals on items which I did not personally want to keep, but which I knew I could resell swiftly for a profit. More often than not when I went into pawn shops or checked newspaper classified ads instead of finding the pre-World War II Martin and Gibson guitars mandolins, and banjos I was seeking I would uncover Gibson and Fender electric guitars or archtop jazz guitars which in the early to mid 1960s were priced at extreme bargains even by the standards of that time and which would seem ridiculously cheap by today's standards. At first I considered many of these instruments to be nuisance byproducts, but it didn't take long before I realized that it was these instruments that could fund my collecting addiction.

Finding fine vintage electric guitars, archtop jazz guitars, mandolins, and banjos involved absolutely zero extra labor. As long as I was already checking music stores, pawn shops, and classified advertising as well as all the bulletin boards at school in my searches for vintage acoustic collectibles I automatically turned up whatever else was in my path. It might be likened to the example of a prospector who sets out looking for gold and starts panning gravel in a promising looking stream who soon discovers that for every nugget of gold he encounters he finds a ton of copper nuggets and perhaps a ton or more of turquoise which he sets aside in separate piles. At the end of the month the prospector may have hundreds of tons of clean sifted gravel, several tons of copper and turquoise and perhaps as little as a quarter ounce of gold. He might soon realize that he's commercial gravel, copper, and turquoise dealer and a hobbyist gold miner.

In the early 1960s there were no books or magazines offering comprehensive information on vintage

Photo credit, Vincent Ricardell.

49

instruments. While today there are hundreds of books and websites offering extensive information, in the early 1960s were virtually no sources information other than talking to dealers who had been handling these instruments for years, and contacting the manufacturers who at that time were usually not in a position to offer extensive information. It was possible, for example, to contact the Martin Guitar Company and find the date of particular instrument, but there weren't even published serial number lists available. While reliable information was scarce at the time, I soon found that the same systematic approach to zoology was perfectly adapted to a systematic study of fretted instruments. To this day I examine guitars, mandolins, and banjos in virtually the same manner I look at reptiles and other zoological specimens. Although my personal interest in fretted musical instruments was almost strictly pre-World War II acoustic models, the same systematic approach work equally well for learning about the electric instruments I encountered.

When I started at the University of Chicago in 1963 the Folklore Society concerts featured only acoustic music. They went so far as to prohibit use of any electric instruments on stage. This seems ironic today, especially in view of the fact that being on the south side of Chicago the University was surrounded by neighborhoods where some of the finest R&B players in the world lived and worked, but the University community and the affluent suburban communities at that time had remarkably little contact with the vibrant Chicago R&B scene.

When I first met Michael Bloomfield he played acoustic blues. He was a wonderfully talented musician, but it was not until he joined the Butterfield Blues Band that I heard him play single note on an electric guitar. Although the University of Chicago Folklore Society had totally ignored the R&B scene prior to Butterfield, the Butterfield band was an overnight sensation on the campus. Once the barrier had been broken the Folklore Society was soon sponsoring concerts on campus featuring artists such as Muddy Waters, Little Richard, Buddy Guy, Howling Wolf, and numerous others.

Bloomfield's first electric guitar with the Butterfield band was a vintage Fender Telecaster. In the mid-1960s no solid body electric was truly old, but Bloomfield was keenly aware that the early models were very different sounding than the new ones available at that time. He not only used vintage instruments in preference to new ones, but was very vocal stating his preferences.

Prior to Bloomfield playing the Telecaster early Telecasters were readily available for no more than $75, but within a matter of a couple of months after he joined the Butterfield band using the Telecaster these same guitars sold for as much as $500. He soon switched from the Telecaster to a 1954 gold top Les Paul with P-90 single coil pickups and a wraparound stud mounted bridge. I observed within a matter of weeks Telecasters went down in price and 54 gold top Les Pauls went from being readily available for under hundred dollars to costing $500-$600. I was very actively seeking Les Paul guitars on the south side of Chicago where many pawnbrokers and the public were unaware of the trend and taking them to the north side of Chicago as well as on the University campus where I could sell them profitably or trade them for instruments I wanted for my personal collection.

While Bloomfield was using the 1954 gold top Les Paul model I heard players I knew comment that it was too bad that Gibson had ever abandoned that design in favor of the late 1950s sunburst style. Several players I knew well assured me that the humbucking pickups sounded sickly sweet and lacked the bite of the P-90 pickups and that the tune-o-matic bridge and stop tailpiece killed sustain and didn't have the tone of the stud mounted wraparound bridge. As long as Bloomfield was playing on a gold top model the white musicians I knew who played R&B were fixated on what he used.

After he had been playing the gold top 54 model for a while Mike mentioned to me that he would like to get one of the sunburst ones with humbucking pickups. Although on the rare occasions when I had encountered one they were relatively inexpensive, even in the mid-1960s when these were not old instruments they were still very rare. Sunburst Les Pauls made from mid-1958 through 1960 as well as early Flying V and Explorer guitars were not a great commercial success when they were new so very few music stores ordered them. I was unable to find one on short notice for Mike, but he was fortunate enough to be able to trade his 54 Les Paul to Dan Erlewine for a 1959 burst. Within a matter of weeks some of the same people who told me that Les Pauls with that humbucking pickups sounded sickly sweet and that the tune-o-matic bridge and stop tailpiece killed sustain could no longer remember ever having said such a thing. Although Mike Bloomfield never had a hit record on par with the Rolling Stones, Eric Clapton, or numerous other performers, during the time when I was a student at the University of Chicago from 1963 through 1967, in my opinion, he was the single most important electric guitar player who influenced what other musicians wanted to play. Eric Clapton, Keith Richards, and John Sebastian had sunburst Les Pauls as early or earlier than Bloomfield, but they switched from one guitar to another rather than settling on the sunburst Les Paul as Bloomfield did. When Bloomfield started to play with Butterfield using an old Telecaster thousands of other musicians took note and wanted vintage electric guitars rather than new and especially sought old Telecasters. I saw a little evidence that old Les Pauls had any special vintage or significant monetary appeal until Bloomfield got his 1954 gold top after which within a matter of weeks I was getting numerous inquiries from people seeking them. When he played his 1954 gold top I wasn't getting inquiries for Sunburst Les Pauls, but once he switched to the burst inquiries rolled in immediately.

During Bloomfield's tenure with Butterfield Gibson was no longer making Les Paul guitars. Although it soon became very clear that there was a strong demand for Les Paul guitars, Gibson did not respond until 1968 when they introduced a gold top model with P-90 pickups resembling a 1956 model guitar rather than a sunburst guitar resembling the 1959 model that Bloomfield and tens of thousands of R&B players were seeking. Most of the new generation of players seeking vintage Les Paul guitars barely knew who Les Paul was and were not in any way trying to study or imitate the music he played. I vividly remember receiving a call from a person wanting a Les Paul guitar pronouncing it Les Paul in the French pronunciation. He was quite shocked to find when I told him that Les Paul was a person and that the guitar and the name had nothing in common with the French pronunciation.

The Les Paul guitar was not originally designed for R&B or rock music, but like many great instruments which have stood the test of time it has gone on to prove itself as an incredibly versatile instrument capable of a wide variety of expression. Although the sunburst Les Paul Standards of mid-1958 through 1960 were not a great commercial success when new, they have gone on to be among the most influential and valuable electric guitars ever made in the history of the instrument.

— George Gruhn

Serial # 9 2319. Submitted by:
Uncle Lou's Classic Guitars, Inc.

Gorgeous late '59 with light flame, serial # 9 2319, very slightly faded showing nearly all of its original deep-cherry sunburst color, in excellent condition. Beneath the nickel covers are double-white and zebra PAF's which is pretty common for bursts in this serial number range. This guitar is a factory 2nd, having a '2' stamped into the headstock above the serial number. Most likely because of the 'beauty mark' by the bridge pickup, which is also why this burst is called 'Cindy' as in Cindy Crawford.

Serial # 9 0691. Here's some provenance for this particular burst. The top left photo was taken in 1974 shortly after the purchase from the original owner for $270.00. The top right photo shows how it looks today.

Serial # 9 1978. *A total fade lemon color '59 with a very pretty face. Photo credit, Richard Henry Guitars.*

Mick Ralphs

"I had the great pleasure of meeting Vic this summer, whilst out on tour with Bad Company. He has, without doubt, the finest collection of Bursts I have ever seen. Not only that, he was gracious enough to give me one of his special run 59' reissues, called the Shadows burst- its a fantastic guitar, Gibson is certainly making the most accurate reissues to date this year. The future of the original Bursts are assured--having owned several over the years, there is no doubt in my mind, that they really are the Holy Grail of the electric guitar, and nothing comes close in terms of old wood, craftsmanship, tone and playability. I only wish I could find and afford one now. The search goes on!"

— *Mick Ralphs*

A young Mike Bauer playing his '59 burst in the late 1960's. This guitar was later bought by J. Geils.

Serial # 9 2074. Nicknamed " The African", this beauty is an African jewel...Vintage guitar dealer Dave Hinson from Killer Vintage is pictured with this exquisite burst.

Here's a photo of Les Paul's personal 1961 SG Les Paul thanks to Rumbleseat Music. The two pickup design was found only on SG LP Standards. The model pictured here is a two pickup SG LP Custom with a full face pickguard. Quite a rare piece. The Les Paul Model went through a drastic body design in 1961 and Les's name was taken off this model in early 1963.

Serial # 9 0592 (left) & 9 1854 (right)

Robby Krieger

My first Les Paul was a 54 black beauty {which Gibson is finally getting around to making a signature model of}. That was in 1966. I was mostly using SGs. At that time there was no such thing as "collectable guitars. If one got old, you bought a new one. In about 1975, I was playing a gig in Boston I think, and playing as the second act was Ann Peebles [I cant stand the rain] Her guitar player was a white guy whose name was Robert Johnson. That was kind of weird, but what really got my attention was his guitar. He had the most beautiful Les Paul sunburst id ever laid eyes on. It had the flames from hell and was in perfect condition. I asked if he wanted to sell it and he said he'd let it go for $3000. I told him he was nuts, and no used guitar was worth that much. Besides not buying land in Venice beach in the early 80s, that was the biggest mistake I ever made. I'm sure Vic knows who has that LP today and Ill bet it's worth over $300,000. I don't buy guitars as investments because I know ^d never sell them, would be too painful, but I wish I had bought that one! About 8 years ago, my buddy Al Jackson called me about a guitar he had seen at Guitar Center, Hollywood. Al and I had been disappointed with Gibson's attempts to make a really true copy of the 60 Les Paul, They did a great job of making it look right, but couldn't quite capture that sound. So we decided to try it ourselves. Al is something of a mad scientist, and had been studying every old guitar he could find. He could be found most days at the guitar shop with his ohmmeter, testing pickup magnets, scouring the internet for what kind of glue they used to use, what kind of wood, etc. We just couldn't believe that it was so hard to make a guitar that sounded as good as the old ones. Anyway we got a bit sidetracked and never finished the project, but haven't given up. Anyway I went down to the store where I was introduced to the "Burst Brothers ", Dave Belzer and Drew Berlin. Notice that both their names can be abbreviated D B, {don't know what that means, but made me suspicious] Belzer and I have become golf buddies, and Drew is the reason I'm in this book...Thank you Drew. So they showed me the guitar and I noticed that it was really light. pretty unusual for a LP. It had some nice color and played really well. We christened it the "Kriegerburst and the rest is history. For me, the Les Paul will always be how an electric guitar should look; something about the shape just looks right. So Robert Johnson, if your reading this, Ill give you $4000 for that guitar!

— Robby Krieger

Serial # 0 8141. *Absolutely gorgeous late '60 with the typical wide-flat neck profile of the era, showing a very translucent tangerine sunburst over a bright yellow center, with a deep book-matched pinstripe top, in excellent condition. The original nickel covers were removed to reveal double-white & zebra PAF's, and at 8.3 pounds, it's wonderfully lightweight. Submitted by: Uncle Lou's Classic Guitars, Inc.*

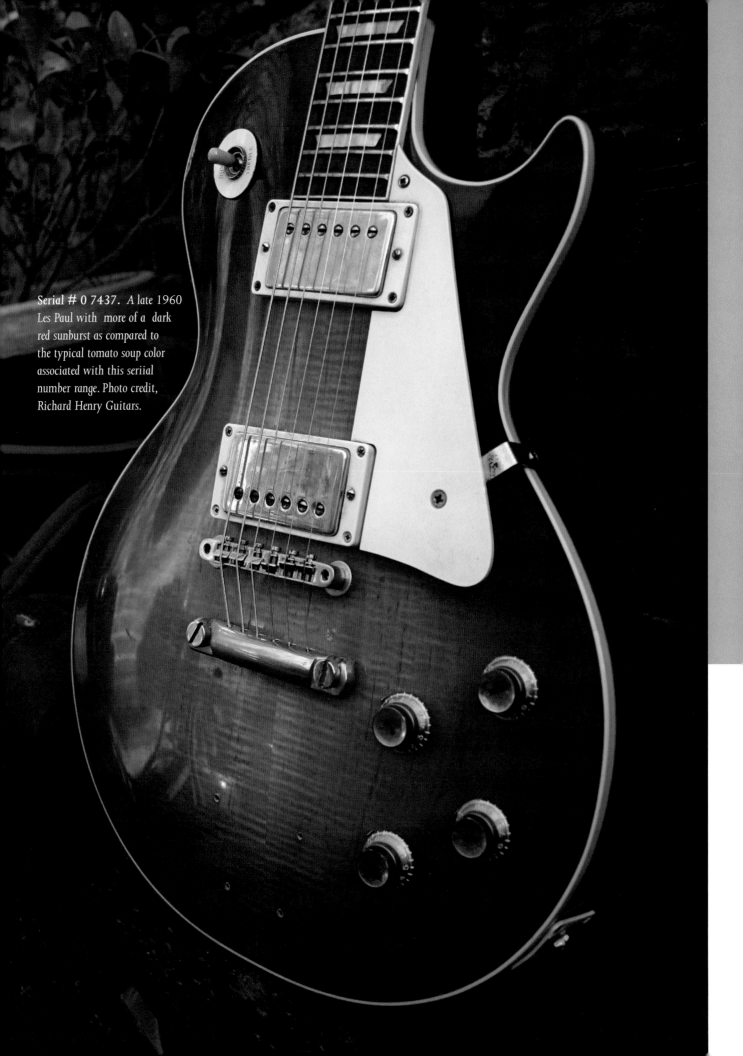

Serial # 0 7437. A late 1960 Les Paul with more of a dark red sunburst as compared to the typical tomato soup color associated with this seriial number range. Photo credit, Richard Henry Guitars.

Serial # 0 0264. Photo credit, Rumbleseat Music

A Gem Down Under

Drop-dead gorgeous early '60, serial # 0 0264, all '59 specs with a fat neck profile, beautiful cherry sunburst finish, over deep & wide irregular flames...among the best I've ever seen. I found it while surfing some online classifieds in 1998 and made an offer based on crappy photos the owner had sent me. He accepted my offer but wanted to be paid in cash which left me no choice but to hop on several planes and make my way from NYC to Australia. It was quite a schlep, but as you can see, this guitar was well worth the monumental effort it took to get it.

— Uncle Lou's Classic Guitars, Inc.

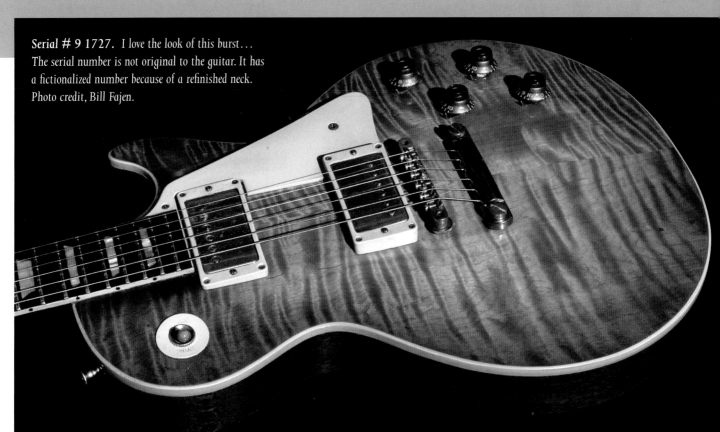

Serial # 9 1727. I love the look of this burst...
The serial number is not original to the guitar. It has
a fictionalized number because of a refinished neck.
Photo credit, Bill Fajen.

Serial # 0 1930. This burst was bought from Norm's Rare Guitars and has resided in Germany since 1979.

Serial # 0 1504. Left handed Sunburst Les Paul's are as rare as hen's teeth..Notice the dots in the binding on the treble side of the neck.This would be the same as on the bass side also. This occurrence only happens on left handed models.

Serial # 9 0878. This burst has an exceptionally beautiful color with mild wide flame.

Serial # 9 0881. 1959 Gibson Les Paul
Standard nicknamed "The Bearded Lady."

Serial # 0 7592. *A late '60 burst with a typical era sunburst color and mild figuring. This guitar was sold to Kirk Hammett from Metallica. Photo credit, Richard Henry Guitars.*

Ray Gomez

Finally sitting down and writhing about my Original Les Paul Sunburst experiences. Nice to write this for burst passionate Vic DaPra on a plane to NYC from Europe with no distractions at 37000 feet with the warm sun coming thru the window.. First of all,thank you to the GREAT legendary guitarist and designer of the Les Paul guitar, Mr Les Paul! For me the love affair started with Eric Clapton in his John Mayall days,and then Fresh Cream. I instantly fell in love with "Hideway",and went about reproducing that sound with any guitar and any amp..that was the goal! Of course we know that many other classic blues/Rock players used that guitar as well. It made everybody look good too,the design was really sexy...the size,the shape the toggle switch at the top, the binding,cream guard and pickups contours...sweet! The heavy flame thing was never really my thing..i just liked the overall guitar look.. In fact, I never really cared for the strong flames. I kinda liked the plainer, with some flame. Page's guitar looked very desirable to me. Also,the combination of that guitar with Marshall Amps was to me the total package. To me it blew away the Fender,getting that saxophone kinda growl,and playing with the nuances.. unmatchable! Eric with Mayall and early Cream was IT to me...it set the standard for the Classic Blues Rock tone forever, aside of course from the alternative, the stratocaster Blues Rock sound, set by Mister James Marshall Hendrix. I got my first Burst in 1975. I was in Heaven. A Tobacco burst with a factory custom ordered Star inlay on the left of the headstock. A great strat and a great Paul. I was ready for the world! As if by miracle,great sessions came in almost immediately after with some of the greatest players of all times. Fusion/ blues/Rock lovers keep reminding me of the "Classic recordings" I have made with that guitar. Such as "White Night" with Narada Michael Walden, "The Dancer" and the "Live 76/77" with Stanley Clarke. I later got a 59, more orangey/ red which was thicker sounding, and ended up on more "classic recordings":"Opening suite, part One" on the "Awakening" album and "Oneness Cry" on the "I cry I smile" album, both records by Narada Michael Walden. Those "Burst tones" are heavenly when handled correctly with soul and maximum taste,as many of you know, and the great Blues and Rock players ALL know this. That guitar is a true Miracle! Thank you Les, and Thank you Vic for this book to be written, and for all the joy this guitar has brought and will keep on bringing! Blessings to all.

— *Ray Gomez ;-)*

1958 Burst

My 1958 Burst (Serial # 8 6738) was the third Burst that I purchased, although ironically, I learned later on from the dealer that it was actually the first Burst that I almost bought until I became concerned that it had too much wear on the back and neck. I backed away from it as a novice collector at that time, before I understood the meaning of mojo! This guitar has a very aggressive bridge pickup that is quintessential rock, and a full bodied neck pickup. It was obviously played a lot! Its 4-latch case has a decal of a crest for Zeta Beta Tau, a fraternity for the City of College of New York, so I imagine this guitar saw a lot of action at college gigs! These 1958 Bursts have a beautiful color that is hard to describe, and this one has faded to a beautiful Teaburst with thin checking across the entire top and a bit of greening where the arm rests. It is the heaviest of my Bursts, weighing in over 9 lbs. Everyone who has played this guitar is blown away by its tone!

Mike Slubowski

Serial # 9 1156.

Tak Matsumoto

Championed in his homeland as the most renowned guitarist in all of Asia, Tak Matsumoto is best known as songwriter, guitarist and producer of Japanese rock duo, B'z. Formed in 1988, Tak and vocalist, Koshi Inaba have released many albums and singles over the course of their career, continuing to top the charts, while holding the record of 45 consecutive #1 single debuts on Japan's Oricon Single Chart. B'z have sold over 80 million CDs in Japan alone, making them the best-selling artist in Japanese history.

Besides releasing a long line of number one singles and albums in Japan, B'z are known for their dynamic live shows. In 2011, B'z completed a sold-out North American tour, ending with an unforgettable show with rock band, Linkin Park to raise money for victims of the Japan tsunami and earthquake. They ended the year with a sold-out dome tour in Japan, including 3 nights at the famed Tokyo Dome with 600,000 fans in attendance.

Under the recommendation of Steve Vai, B'z were inducted into the Hollywood Rock Walk in 2007 as the first Asian artist. As a world acclaimed six-string virtuoso, Tak joined legendary guitarists Jimmy Page, Joe Perry, Ace Frehley and Slash, to become the fifth guitarist in the world to have his own Gibson signature model, the 'Tak Matsumoto Les Paul.' In addition, Tak has his own original model, the 'Tak Matsumoto Double Cutaway,' and has released 7 models so far.

Beginning his career as a session musician, Tak's exposure to a myriad of musical styles molded his own unique blend, by incorporating elements of jazz, blues, classical, metal, rock and ska. He released the critically acclaimed instrumental albums, Hana and Dragon From The West, to rave reviews for their powerful flowing melodies and evocative imagery.

In 2010, Tak joined forces with jazz guitarist, Larry Carlton and released the album, Take Your Pick. Drawing upon their knowledge and different musical backgrounds, Tak and Larry blended their Eastern and Western guitar styles to create a truly magical and unique album. After a successful tour of Taiwan, Hong Kong and Japan, Take Your Pick won the Grammy for Best Pop Instrumental Album at the 53rd Grammy Awards in February 2011.

Tak released his latest solo album Stirings Of My Soul world.

I started playing guitar when I was 15 years old and my first guitar was a Japanese copy of a Les Paul. I wanted to be like Jimmy Page just as every guitar kid wanted to be. I believe I got this guitar in 1993 and I never dreamed that I would own an actual '59 Les Paul Standard. This guitar is a very fundamental instrument and was key in triggering the beginning of rock'n'roll. I'm very proud to own this guitar and I truly appreciate the great work of Mr.Les Paul.

— Tak Matsumoto

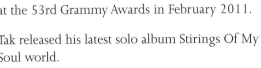

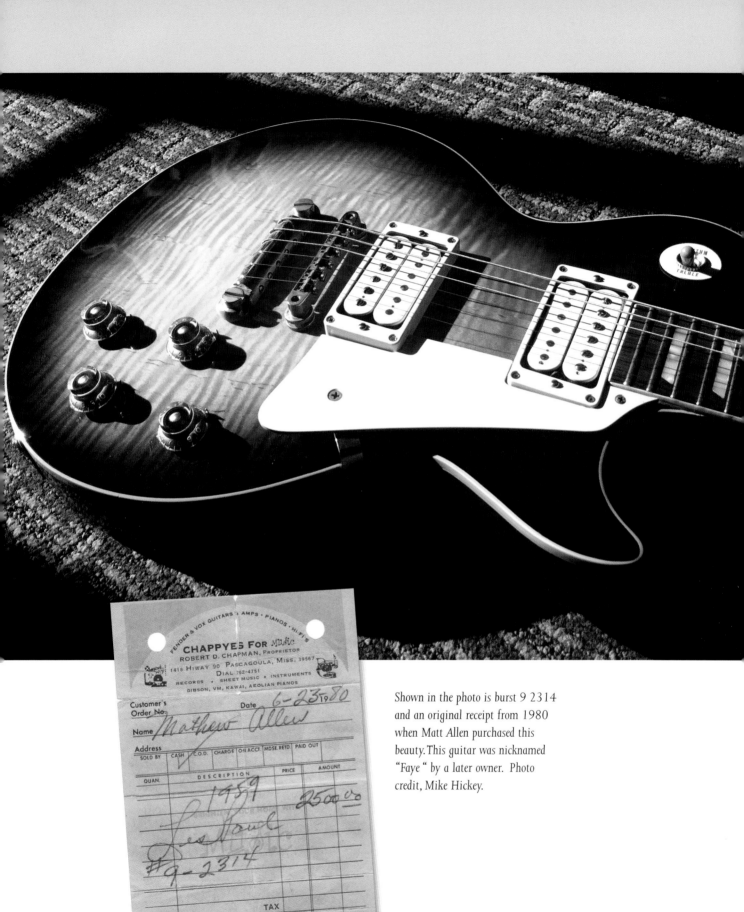

Shown in the photo is burst 9 2314 and an original receipt from 1980 when Matt Allen purchased this beauty. This guitar was nicknamed "Faye" by a later owner. Photo credit, Mike Hickey.

Serial # 0 0256. *An early '60 with flecking in the top and faint pinstripe curl. The color and fade on this particular guitar is just gorgeous.*

Serial # 8 5501. *Here's Keith Scott's beautiful '58 burst on Mike Hickey's work bench backstage at a Joe Bonamassa gig. Keith played guitar in the Bryan Adams band.*

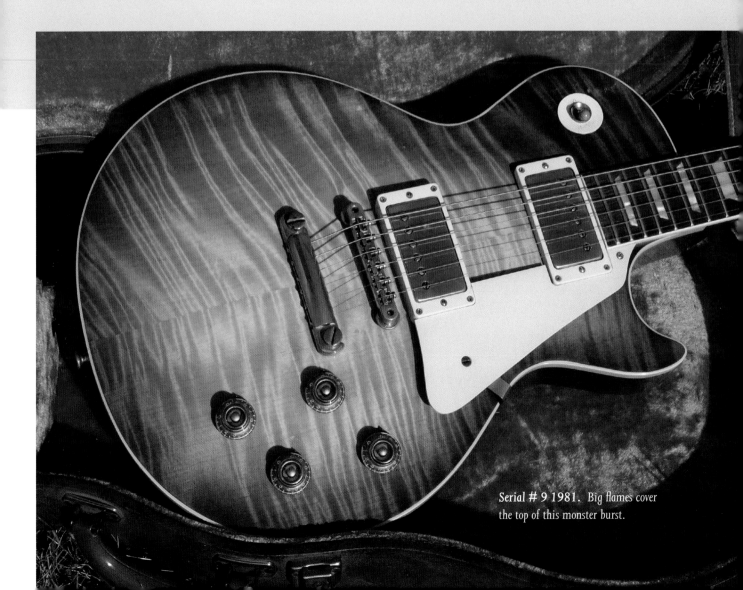

Serial # 9 1981. *Big flames cover the top of this monster burst.*

Serial # 9 0337. Catching a few rays and showing off its original tags , this burst was purchased from Drew Berlin and now resides in France.

Serial # 9 0655 This faded out '59 is owned by Rick Nielsen.

One of Rick's many main stage guitars..

All Rick Nielsen photos courtesy of Mike Graham.

BURST? BURST? BURST?

You mean a Gibson Les Paul Standard Sunburst?" When I think
of the term "burst", I picture a balloon, a tire, a dam burst, burst
out laughing, some kind of candy, burst thru the door I picture a
holiday feast having had way too much to eat and then bursting at
the seams, Or, being a patriotic guy that I am, "the bombs bursting
in air" but when it comes to my friend Vic DaPra, I can always make
an exception, after all it is his book, and HE can call it a "burst" or
anything he wants. but to me, they'll always be the "Gibson Les Paul
Standard Sunburst", and that's all I have to say about that!

— Rick Nielsen

Serial # 8 6753. My father bought this guitar for me in 1970. We were at a jam session and some guy wanted to sell it. My father gave him $100.00 for the guitar and an Epiphone amp. Submitted by Dan Boone.

Robbert van der Ende

It was in 2006 on a sunny day in August when I was working in my guitar store, 'Max Guitar' in The Hague, The Netherlands when a guy of around 40 years old walked in. He was carrying an older, rough looking black Les Paul style case. I was alone in the store, which was still a small one man operation at that time. He introduced himself and told me he had an older guitar that he wanted to show me. I presumed him to be the owner of the guitar and he told me that the guitar in the case used to belong to his father who had passed away not so long ago and that he thought it to be a special instrument. Now, you have to understand that when you own a guitar store you get this all the time… people convinced they have a very special guitar to show you. Most of the time of course only special to them. Which is also the charm of having a store like this and beats having a computer- of a shoe store I believe.

The original owner with his burst in 1969

Since the case was black and did not show any specific 'Gibson' or other markings I had no immediate clue to what kind of guitar he was preparing to show me. Not recognizing the case being any particular brand at all I was expecting nothing in particular, least of all a Burst! But of course I was curious. Opening an old guitar case is like opening a birthday present. The excitement, the smell. But when I opened this case I was stunned, I couldn't believe my eyes. The guitar in the case appeared to be a late 1960 Les Paul. I say appeared as I must have checked the serial at least three or four times. A little more than excited I launched into an internal conversation with myself: "This must be a 1960 Les Paul….at least it has all the hallmarks of one. It can't be, but still it is…or is it? Wow! Of course it had the serial number starting with 0. It was rather a high number …in this case 011167 indicating that it was a guitar produced in late 1960. The retolexed case had been a perfect camouflage so far; as a weathered brown Lifton case would have been a dead giveaway from the

start. A perfect dark burst with all infamous tomato-soup-red still present, a great spaghetti flame top and great, rich weather checking. The instrument seemed to have been in the case for years as the strings were rusty. The tuners had been replaced with Schaller locking tuners (!) and the strap holders had been exchanged with strap locks of the same brand. But apart from this and a replaced bridge, as this had caved in to string pressure quite some time ago, the guitar was totally original. The old and shrunken Klusons were still in the case compartment. The guitar didn't play well at all, the frets were a little corroded and the string action was far too low. Some of the pots were stuck and the guitar was greasy. If I didn't know what this was exactly it would have been just another old and dirty, smelly guitar. Due to the unlikelihood of finding such an instrument I was still in doubt if it was in fact the real deal. But of course it was. I asked the owner if he minded if I would make pictures of the guitar. He agreed. I still have these and I think I just wanted to make sure when I woke up the next day I could prove to myself that it hadn't been a dream. I asked the guy if he knew what type of instrument this was and he nodded. "My father Jan, played this instrument all his life. He was a musician in a jazz trio working on cruise ships performing jazz standards. Picture a three piece suit, bow tie, mirror balls, 'Besame Mucho', 'Blue Moon' and 'Autumn leaves'… the works! He ordered the guitar from Gibson and received the guitar in 1961 and has been playing it ever since. (see picture) Later when Gibson prepared this guitar to be re-issued in the Collectors Choice series, Edwin Wilson from Gibson confirmed this most likely to be a special order guitar due to the finish being Dark burst and the top being the nice, tight spaghetti flame that it is. The owner continued: "When my father

died I inherited the guitar but due to its value I never actually dared to play it on stage. I stored the guitar inside our upright piano for safe keeping. I changed the tuners because the old ones were actually dysfunctional." I was blown away and impressed by the sheer history that this guitar and its case 'oozed'. The thick weather checking, the fatty, greasy dirt on the instrument, the worn plastic parts, the grooves in the fingerboard, the rusty strings making a grinding noise over the corroded frets. Nothing like the type of aging, however well executed by the likes of Tom Murphy. This was REAL! This guitar had lived a full life! It actually 'lived' so much that in the early seventies the case was already looking very battered and the lacquer was starting to check in some areas, even so much so that Jan's band members complained to Jan about this fact and told him that this 'look' was inappropriate for the image of the band. They wanted a more shiny, undamaged look for the guitar. Why didn't he buy another one they wondered? When Jan refused the drummer of the trio decided to 'surprise' Jan and re-tolexed the battered brown Lifton case to its present black condition and took a can of varnish and a paintbrush and actually varnished the worst weather checking hoping for a more smooth result. Enough to make one cringe! I asked the son of the owner if this guitar was for sale, fearing that he actually might say yes and present me with a high asking price. However much I wanted to own this great piece of history, any transaction was very likely to involve an amount money that I didn't have at that time anyway. He said that he didn't want to sell the guitar as it had been his father's and that he was very attached to it and its history. I was disappointed and relieved at the same time… a strange sensation. Probably because I probably could not grasp actually owning what is generally seen as the holy grail in the guitar world as we know it. These are generally guitars that other people own. In any case: It had been a pleasant meeting and we want on to 'talk guitars' and discuss the value of this guitar and guitars in general and I asked the owner to contact me if he ever wanted to sell it. He said he would as he might want to redecorate his house at a later point in time. We said our goodbyes and we both went about our business. In the years following our meeting I occasionally saw the owner and he actually purchased an amp and a few guitars from me, including a LP reissue that he played instead of the 1960 LP in fear of it getting stolen or broken. I asked him a few times if he still owned THE guitar and he said it was safely sitting back home in the upright piano. I never put pressure on him to sell me the guitar. It was clear he would either never sell the guitar or contact me when he was ready. It was never about money for him, that much was clear. The guitar would stay in the piano for the next few years. During one of his visits to the store he told me a great anecdote about how his father 'stored' this guitar. In the time his Father played the guitar on the cruise ships he would come back to port after weeks of being at sea and drive home in his imported Russian Lada and park the car on the driveway next to his house. He would leave the guitar in the unlocked trunk or on the back seat of the car and when anybody would ask him if he wasn't afraid anybody might steal it, he would answer: "Why would anybody be interested in an old guitar like this?". His son went on to tell me that at one time during the nineteen seventies in the middle of the night the house was on fire and while most of the house actually was burning down with all their musical equipment inside it, the Burst was sitting 'safely' in the Lada in its usual place. The fire department, whilst in the midst of fighting the blaze, decided to tow the car into the street because they were afraid it might catch on fire. The next day when the smoke had cleared they found the car exactly where the firefighters towed it…in the middle of the street, unlocked with the Burst still on the back seat. It was October 2012 more than six years after the initial meeting when the owner contacted me and told me he wanted to meet. I was anxious to know what he would have to say and afraid that the amount he would ask for the burst would be well above my means although my guitar store had grown considerably since then. But somehow I also had a very good feeling about this. We met the next week at the owners house and we had a great talk about the guitar, it's history and more. The owner told me that he also had a good feeling about selling the guitar to me and that he appreciated very much that I never pressured him about selling it. I told him that I wanted him to name his price. He told me his figure and after some research of all the parts and some healthy consideration, deliberation and checking of the old savings account I told him I would gladly buy his guitar. We proceeded to make the financial arrangements and then I was the proud owner of one of the illusive 635 or so Bursts produced in the year of 1960. It was and is a euphoric and almost unreal feeling that is hard to describe. What happened after that when I made it public here in the Netherlands is even harder to describe. Articles were written in several guitar magazines. The guitar was featured in some local and national TV programs and also compared on live TV with later reissues. The Gibson Custom division expressed an interest in reissuing the guitar and will do so as Gibson Custom Collectors choice #18 affectionately nicknamed: the Dutch Burst. Edwin Wilson and Thom Fowle of the Custom division came to the Netherlands in April 2013 to measure and photograph this guitar.

Robbert van der Ende

Serial # 9 2208.
"Greeny." Photo credit,
Richard Henry.

Kirk Hammett

I first got to know Kirk Hammett when he bought a 1960 Les Paul
I took down to the Reading Rock Festival when Metallica were
headlining one year. James Hetfield also later bought a 1958 burst and a
60's Flying V from me so occasionally I reach out to them when I think
I may have something of interest. When I first took delivery of 'Greeny',
forgetting it's history, controversy and the superstition that surrounding
it, I was immediately struck again by how good the top looked and
then how great the guitar actually sounded. It has a wider dynamic
range than many other bursts I've played and the bridge pickup has
so much bite to it that it almost sounds possessed. I emailed Kirk
who immediately got back to me said he'd be in London in a couple
of weeks and that he'd really like to see the guitar. So the day before
Metallica were due to play the Glastonbury Festival I took 'Greeny' over
to the band's hotel. Kirk didn't have an amp in his room so I had to
call a friend who lived nearby who kindly came over with an original

vintage Marshall 18w combo so we could plug in. There was no doubt in my mind that he wasn't ever going
to not buy the guitar after he'd played it through that amp. After twenty minutes of playing and some earlier
pursuasion from a certain Mr Jimmy Page who had told Kirk ''That's THE one to have'', the deal was done.
When the band returned to the UK a week later, Kirk Hammett became the third high profile guitar player to
take 'Greeny', possibly the most notorious 59 Les Paul ever, back on the road. On it's debut gig with Metallica,
'Greeny' made it's first major public comeback to over 40,000 rock fans at a show in Prague.

— Richard Henry
www.richardhenryguitars.com

Photo credit, Richard Henry.

Serial # 0 7166. This fantastic example of a 1960 Burst was originally owned by a gentleman from a coal mining town in Pennsylvania who basically only played it in church on Sundays and took excellent care of it. It exhibits the typical appointments that one would expect from a 1960 Les Paul, such as the thinner, faster playing neck profile and the bright red color along the edges of the Burst. Unplugged, the old-growth Honduran mahogany and the gorgeous maple top work in tandem with the single piece mahogany neck and Brazilian rosewood finger board to yield uncompromising and open resonance. When plugged in, the PAF's make it known loud and clear why they are considered to be the souls of these guitars. And it's not just us that are crazy about this guitar, good friends of CME such as Steve Miller, Eric Johnson and Joe Bonamassa have played it and have agreed that this is one hell of an instrument…Daniel Escauriza.

Bernie Marsden

I purchased my first Standard in 1973, a converted Gold Top from around 54, refinished by the legendary Dick Knight for me, it had binding around the headstock, that looked original!

The Beast was my second Standard, I found out recently that the person I bought it from had bought it from Andy Fraser, who got it from Paul Kossoff, who had got it from Eric Clapton! And three weeks ago Andy Summers told a guitar magazine that he thinks Eric bought it from him, so quite a lineage for this guitar.

But to me it is the sound of course, Joe Bonamassa plays it a lot, he said it is the loudest guitar unplugged and plugged in he has ever played.

What can I add to all the great words written about the Les Paul Standard, well without this one I would not be writing these words!

The guitar is simply "The Beast"

— Bernie Marsden

(above) Photo credit, Dan Bull.

Serial # 9-1914. 1959 Purchased by me in 1974 in London, used on all Whitesnake recordings, "Here I Go Again" written with this guitar.

Serial # 9 1089. 1959 Gibson Les Paul Standard, faded cherry sunburst over strong pencil-wide flames. The expertly book-matched top almost appears to be one piece of maple and lights up from either side.

Serial # 9 0676. They just keep coming...another "killer" burst from the 9 0600 run. **Photo credit, Mike Hickey.**

Serial # 9 0903. Photo credit, Richard Henry.

Hamilton guitar stand ad featuring an original
Flying V and Ed King's 1960 'burst 0 7441.

Serial # 9 0929. *Another entry from the 9 0900 series with strong color remaining. One would have to wonder why most of the bursts in this serial number range have retained their color so well. Also, the color leans more to a plum color rather than cherry sunburst It seems Gibson was experimenting with their color and spray patterns for this series of bursts.*

Serial # 9 0289

Charlie Daughty

I fell in love with Les Pauls at a very early age. My dad, inadvertently, was the first one to get me bitten by the vintage bug. He bought me my first guitar for $100. It was a used 1964 Gibson SG Special. After playing new ones, I could tell there was something different, and to my ears better, about the old ones. Around 1983, after graduating law school, I bought my first burst, a flamey 1960, with a few issues, for the princely sum of $5000. Gosh I wish I still had that guitar! However, as I have often done in my vintage quest, I traded it, and some other stuff, and cash, to upgrade to a 59 burst. And the hunt continued from there. I loved the thrill of the chase almost as much as I did the ownership of them. Almost every burst I've owned, I acquired through this "upgrade" method. In fact, my all time favorite, "it'll go to my grave with me" guitar, "Nicky," a 59, was acquired from my best friend Ronny Proler. Although he's owned a boatload of the finest bursts on the planet, I never really lusted after any of his until he got Nicky. The first time

I plugged it in, I knew it was the burst for me. I was relentless. In addition to playing the best friend card, I pestered, cajoled and begged him, until he finally relented and let me trade him too many really good guitars for it. I'm embarrassed to admit what all I traded him to get that guitar, but I've never once regretted it. It's "my" guitar. I love everything about it; the top, the tone, the neck… everything.

I'll never tire of vintage Les Pauls. Bursts are so special, and so unique. Each one is different in tone and personality. One of my favorite things about burst collecting is the burst community. I've gotten to meet so many great guys who share the same lust that I do. Almost every burst owner I've ever met is more than happy to share his love and knowledge of these legendary instruments.

I'm hooked for life. My wife says if I have to have an obsession, this is a pretty good one to have.

Yours very truly,

— Charles A. Daughtry'

Serial # 9 1945. Charlie Daughtry's main squeeze "Nicky."

Serial # 9 1982. Nicknamed "The Duke," this amazing burst came out of Canada. Photo Credit, Charlie Daughtry.

Serial # 9 2014. *This stellar burst photo was submitted by Detlef Alder. This particular guitar has been in Germany since the mid 1980's.*

Serial # 9 0889. *Strong color remains on this original bigsby burst. All four coils are white underneath the covers.*

Rick Vito

"At age 15, the first guy I noticed playing a Les Paul with a sunburst finish was one of my greatest idols, Keith Richards. I was transfixed by the sight of it and its small sized body, and I imagined that this was probably the guitar that got all the cool sounds on the Stones records I loved so well. At this time I was a James Burton and Mike Bloomfield style Telecaster man, but in the back of my mind I knew that someday I too would own a guitar like Keith's. Soon after, the buzz started building on Les Pauls after Bloomfield switched to one on the Paul Butterfield album, "East-West," and the word on the street was that this was THE guitar to have. Mike then switched again to a sunburst model, much like Keith's, around about the time Eric Clapton and Peter Green were said to have played this model on the iconic John Mayall blues albums, "Bluesbreakers," and "A Hard Road." The search was definitely on now, and I hit every music and pawn shop within my reach looking for a Les Paul. I had little luck finding one until out of the blue a guy I knew called saying he had one that he wanted to trade

for an SG with humbuckers. I found a good one, bought it and made the trade...I had my first 1957 Les Paul Goldtop Standard with humbuckers!

It was an incredible sounding and playing Paul, and this was my main guitar for a few years, the one I started out my professional career using. Duane Allman played it in my hotel room when I was on tour with Delaney & Bonnie and said he had had one just like it and loved them. Then he opened his case and showed me the UNBELIEVABLY CLEAN sunburst model he had just gotten, and my mouth must have hit the floor. I vowed I would not rest until I had one like this!

That day came around 1978 through Norman Harris at Norman's Rare Guitars. I had written a piece on him and his store in 1976 that was published in Guitar Player magazine (the first article I know of on collecting rare guitars) in which I had wrote the line, "Who would have ever believed that today a Les Paul sunburst would command the astounding price of $2,000!" In just two years since then, the price jumped up to $5,000, but this time I was ready, and I bought my first "Burst," a clean '58 model with mild flame which I used for about seven years until a mortgage and birth of my son forced me to part with it.

I knew I'd get another someday, and I did around '88, again through Norman. This one was five times the cost of my first but it was a real beauty, a cherry '59 with medium flame that was clean as a whistle and sounded like a million. Later I also bought a '60 model with mild flame that looked like it had never been played which later was sold to a major rock star guitarist whose name I will refrain from publicizing.

One day I got a call from Dan Duehren, Norman's partner at the time, saying that another rock star (who also will remain nameless) was parting out his collection and a '59 model was available at a good price.

This one had even been in a Gibson ad, so it had some good provenance as well. I hurried down to the store and saw what was to become the guitar I now own. One chordal strum and a few licks and I instantly knew that this was the best Burst I'd ever played, and so I bought it on the spot. It wasn't the cleanest or "flamiest" by any means, but it had that unmistakeable SOUL that we guitarists spend our lives seeking. Guitars have come and gone in my life, often helping me into great working situations and out of difficult financial periods, but I have vowed if it is humanly possible, I'll never let this Les Paul go.

Today I love to design guitars and even have a Rick Vito Signature model out through my friends at Reverend Guitars of which I'm very proud. I've owned and played just about every guitar I ever wanted. But, a Burst is a Burst, and if you are lucky enough, as I have been, to have the good fortune to own an original Les Paul Sunburst Standard made from 1958 through 1960, then you know that this IS the Holy Grail of electric guitars...the one tried, true, and tested model that all others must respect as "the best."

Perhaps the younger players of today will not fully appreciate this because the guitar idols of their youth may not have been Bloomfield, Clapton, Richards or Green. But I suspect that some in the know will, and a new generation will take up the call when some amazing personality plays an astounding solo on some recording, and announces to the world that "it was played on an old Burst!"

— Rick Vito

Serial # 9 0643. *A first rate photo of a top notch burst perched upon its case.*

Serial # 0 1498. *If you check out page 74 in BURST BELIEVERS 1, you'll see burst 0 1495. If you compare the two photos, you can see these two bursts were produced from the same billet of wood. Two absolutely amazing guitars.*

Serial # 9 1986. *An incredibly flamed '59 out of Canada with an insanely flamed top.*

Serial # 9 0227. *An early '59 that was exported to England & spent most of it's time there until 2009. It has the export dark purple lined case. It now resides with me in Canada. Narration and photo credit, Tony Fewkes.*

Serial # 9 0668. *Another great one from 9 0600 series. The flame on this burst is spectacular.*

Tom Keifer

"The '59 burst has stood the test of time. That tone
is just a part of history on so many amazing records
A burst is really like a classic car. Here to stay!!"

— Tom Keifer

Photo credit: Hannah Keifer

Serial # 9 1156. Another look at this beauty.

Joe Bonamassa

There is little that can be said that hasn't already been said about the iconic 1958, 1959 and 1960 Gibson Les Paul Standard model. They have proven to be and in my opinion will continue to prove for future generations to be the closest instrument modern times has ever produced to the great violin makers of the 17 th and 18 th century. Pictures of these guitars dawned my wall as a kid along with the players that made them famous. Over the past few years its been a real honor to meet and share knowledge and of course guitars with some of the industries founding fathers, legends and passionate collectors. I could never repay the generosity that has been shown to me but I can promise to share them with a younger generation of players to insure these guitars find homes and more importantly stages and records to play on for years to come. Cheers to Vic DaPra for passion ,love and commitment to these great books and to the many generous owners sharing these great pictures and information.

All the best.

— Joe Bonamassa
(certified burst addict 9-1951, 9-1688, 9-0829, 0-7453, 0-7589)

Photo credit, Charlie Daughtry

The "Other Peter Green Burst"

The newspaper ad read "1950's Gibson Les Paul for sale". A short phone call later my friend and I were headed for the nearest Autobahn on-ramp to take us to Duesseldorf. The guitars were offered by a German underwriter for famed British insurer "Lloyds of London".

The year was 1984; vintage Sunburst Les Pauls had made their way past the $5,000 mark in the US and were nearly impossible to find in Europe. "Our" Burst had been stolen in the UK and later recovered in Germany. The price was right, my friend had the cash and off we went with our find, feeling like we had just struck gold A decade earlier Paul Warren, Motown's wunderkind session guitar player in Detroit was busy tracking down vintage Sunburst Les Pauls when he came across the flamiest Burst he'd ever seen, a late1960, owned by a flea market hustler from Drayton Plains, Michigan.

Peter Green and Frank Lucido pose with Peter's newly acquired 1960 Les Paul Standard courtesy of Mick Fleetwood. - Photo by Frank Lucido.

Paul had to have it. In 1975 he finalized the deal and bought it for $2,000.

Shortly thereafter, the Burst's slender neck was destroyed in a collision with a microphone stand during a rehearsal in LA. Luthier Yuris Zeltins, the "Zen master of little details" replicated the neck, using the original logo, fret board and holly veneer but left it without a serial number. A few years and countless recording sessions later, Paul traded the Burst to a collector for a '58 Explorer, but not before swapping the PAF pickups.. Little did we know…

In early 1979, Frank Lucido was teaching high school in Downey, California. His hobby was collecting and dealing vintage guitars. This frequently put him in touch with the who's who of LA's music scene, including Mick Fleetwood of Fleetwood Mac. On one occasion Lucido stuffed 31 guitars into his '71 Cadillac El Dorado and headed for the Mac's rehearsal house to show them to the band. By the time he left he had sold all but 2 guitars, including a flamey '59 Burst that prompted a very memorable response from Christine McVie. "Oooo, a Peter Green guitar!" Mick Fleetwood must have been listening. A few months later Frank Lucido got another call from Mick Fleetwood, who felt the

Peter Green with his flamey late1960 Burst during the late 70's. The guitar , mistaken as a '59 by Peter's biographer Martin Celmins, features a replaced neck without serial number, and PAFs off a '58 Explorer. The reflector knobs had been replaced with Bonnet knobs by Paul Warren - GAB / Redferns / Getty Images.

time had come for Peter Green to own a proper "Peter Green guitar" again. Frank had 4 Bursts at his house, three were killer – near mint, and the fourth was the 1960 he had gotten from Paul Warren. Peter plugged each Burst into a Marshall stack, but instead of tearing into "Green Manalishi" he barely turned it up and strummed an E chord on each for a few seconds. Much to

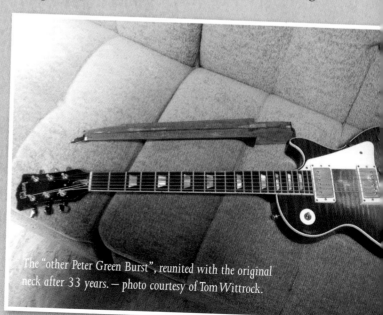

The "other Peter Green Burst", reunited with the original neck after 33 years. – photo courtesy of Tom Wittrock.

The Warren/Green Burst in 2008. The PAFs are long gone. Photo courtesy of Thomas Willemsen.

Lucido's surprise he chose the '60 with the replaced neck over the three '59s because he genuinely preferred it's sound and thin neck reminiscent of Clapton's '60 Burst that Peter had always admired.ick Fleetwood must have been listening. Peter Green didn't rejoin Fleetwood Mac, dashing Mick's hopes once and for all. According to his biographer Martin Celmins, Green was overjoyed to have the Burst, but not long after acquiring it, handed it to a stranger in a hotel elevator, and the guitar ended up in a pawnshop, where it was later recovered. Peter may have recorded with it, possibly on Fleetwood Mac's "Tusk" and his own "White Sky" album but no definitive proof has come to light. Neither Peter or Mick have any recollection about this guitar's fate but it's safe to say that Peter and his Burst made it back to the UK. For his part, Lucido recalls an inquiry from a British guitar dealer in the early '80s regarding the replaced neck of Peter Green's Les Paul. It is unclear who bought and insured it with Lloyds of London but from 1984 forward it's been in the possession of my very fortunate friend.

—Werner Althaus

Serial # 9 0629. Nicknamed "Goldie."

John Peden's photo of vintage guitar dealer Bruce Sandler (circa 1979) at a Texas guitar show. Bruce is shown holding a newspaper ad from which he bought "Goldie"...quite a find!

Serial # 9 2035. *An exquisite '59 in near mint condition with a beautiful three tone sunburst. This burst is owned by Brian Fischer. Photo courtesy of Gordon Miller.*

Serial # 0 1490. 1960 Gibson Les Paul Standard, serial number 0 1490, very nice condition with gorgeous color and flame on two completely different pieces of mismatched maple. But still nice enough to be featured on the cover of Mac Yasuda' 'The Vintage Guitar' volume two. Submitted by Lou Gatanas.

Serial # 0 7617. A magnificent late '60 with a great top. Photo credit, Steve Gornall.

Serial # 8 6895. *A very attractive '58 burst with an impressive top. Photo credit, David Belzer.*

Serial # 9 2185. *A magnificent 100% original '59 burst. Photo credit, Charlie Daughtry.*

Serial # 0 7453.

My 1960 Les Paul Standard story by Phil Keaggy

My first electric guitar was given to me at Christmas 1962 by my brother Dave. It didn't have a name on the headstock, so it was some sort of custom ¾ size cutaway with one pickup. It was most likely designed after a Les Paul Junior model. I loved that little guitar! Dave also gave me a little Orpheus amplifier to go with it. About 2 years later I got a Fender Strat, on which I learned more and more The Strat eventually was traded in for a Mosrite electric. From there I went to a Tele, which was eventually stolen out of our band's van in 1967. I found a Gibson 335 that I really liked and that was my 1st Gibson guitar.

As a tenth grader in 1968 living in both Ohio and So California that year, I discovered many great guitar players and bands. I had heard Michael Bloomfield's guitar work on the Paul Butterfield's albums and also came to find out he played on Bob Dylan's recordings. Maybe that's why I came to play the Tele as that was his main guitar then. I can't remember how it was that I came to discover the Electric Flag's Columbia release ~A Long time Comin in '68 but I loved Mike Bloomfield's guitar work and tones on that LP. The cover showed members of the band and there was a picture of Bloomfield with his Burst Les Paul. I dreamed of having one of those guitars one day, and started playing along with the Flag's recordings in my bedroom.

In the Summer of '68 I started a trio with friends John Sferra and Steve Markulin. We called ourselves the Glass Harp. I bought a 1968 black Les Paul Custom guitar at a local guitar shop in Youngstown Ohio. It was known as the "fretless wonder", as I recall. I had new and larger frets put on the guitar and worked at my tones and style to sound like a little Michael Bloomfield.

I got a Fender Twin Reverb and played as often as I could, learning more all the time.

In 1969 a school mate pal of mine and very good guitarist, Gary Markasky, had a sunburst Les Paul that he was eager to show me. It had a Bigsby tremolo arm and the back had a leather cover, shaped to fit. I guess the previous owner must've had some big belt buckles and wanted to protect the back of the Paul from scratches. How the trade with Gary came about I don't fully remember, but I convinced him to trade our Les Pauls if I threw in the Fender Twin as well. By this time, our bassist Daniel Pecchio joined Glass Harp and we were gigging a lot. We were also playing frequently at a club in Kent Ohio called JBs. A lot of bands played there, but I think Glass Harp played there the most.

The James Gang played at JBs as well.

There were times when Glass harp shared the bill with James Gang at JBs. Joe Walsh became a favorite guitar player of mine. We often jammed Jeff's Boogie by Jeff Beck on stage there, trading licks. I learned a lot from Joe! It was the feeling he put into his playing that moved me the most! When my Les Paul needed some work done on it, Joe loaned me his gold top for a couple of gigs. Soon after that Glass harp was opening for lots of famous bands across the country. We did many dates with Humble Pie as well. Peter Frampton's guitar playing also was inspiring to me, he being a Les Paul man himself. Up to this time, I learned lots of things from records, but to see and spend time with these two players was a great way to learn and I learned a lot. The old 60 Les Paul was my "JY" as it was affectionately known to me and the band, and was in my hands as often I could find the time to play it. Our road manager, Al Pethal, once chased a guy who stole my old Les Paul after a gig at the Columbus Ohio Agora, almost a half mile down High Street till he caught up with him and took back my guitar. I can't recall how that exchange went.

Our band landed a contract with the Decca record label in 1970. I used the 60 Burst on our debut LP Glass Harp. Before that we did some demos recorded in Cleveland which I used that guitar as well. At the time, I was also doing home recordings and have songs where I played that guitar. As I played different Les Pauls that my friends had I wanted one with a little fatter neck. I think the reason being was that I, at the time, was playing a classical guitar and writing songs on it. Perhaps it was the going from that neck to my Paul that made me desire a fatter neck. I ordered a special Les Paul from a local guitar store. The guitar was built in Kalamazoo MI –a beautiful guitar with gold hardware! But, I was disappointed in two things~ It didn't have the thicker neck I had hoped for and it had the Deluxe pickups which weren't the big humbuckers I wanted. I was bummed. I think I took it back and the store sold it to someone else. The store had a new 1971 Deluxe cherry sunburst with the smaller deluxe pickups, but it had the neck I wanted, so–I traded straight, even, my 60 Burst for the 71 Deluxe. I recall the price tag was around $675.00.

I did lots of gigs with Glass Harp and my new Les Paul, and recorded our second LP Synergy in the Summer of 71, not wondering what would become of the old 60 Paul. After a while, I met Virgil Lay who put Gibson humbucker pickups on my 71 Paul. Glass harp played Carnegie Hall in Nov 71 and opened for the Kinks. A live recording was made and after 25 years in the can, the album was released around 1996. It's still a favorite of mine. I played my Les Paul into 2 souped up Twin Reverbs and never used any effects apart from the reverb and vibrato in the Twins.

Around this time, Glass harp did a lot of CA dates and we opened up for Mike Bloomfield in San Francisco. Very excited, I expected to see and hear him with his Les Paul, but that night he played an ES 355 –a fine guitar also. I had hoped, however, to hear that Les Paul in his hands. I played mine of course, and 3 years later ran into Michael at a recording studio in Miami and asked him if he remembered that night. He told me "yea, I do, You're the little guy that played your ass off ! " I took that as a compliment. God rest his soul. I loved Michael's musicianship!

By 1972 we recorded our 3rd studio LP called It Makes Me Glad. Still, my only electric was that 71 Deluxe. It's 2014 and I still own that guitar after 42 years. It still plays great and has the tone I've always loved about Les Pauls.

So what became of the 60 Burst? Well–my family and I moved to Nashville in the Summer of 1989. I was making albums and touring occasionally with bands but mostly doing solo acoustic dates. Having worked with a great Nashville string section on my acoustic album, Beyond Nature, I was introduced to the players. Later I came to find out that the violist's husband was from my hometown of Youngstown Ohio. His name is Larry, a fine musician, and he told me he had the old 60 Sunburst and showed it to me. The Gibson's Custom Shop cleaned it up for him and it played beautifully and looked like a gem! I'm glad it ended up in the hands of someone who could truly appreciate its value and history.

At the age of nineteen, I didn't realize I'd see that guitar again so many years later and that it had become a true classic—a collector's dream guitar!

I truly believe that the Gibson Les Paul has influenced and encouraged so many musicians and helped shape the world of music—both on stage and in the studio.

Way to go Mr Les Paul! What a fine design!

– Phil Keaggy

Photo credit, Anastasia Pantsios

Serial # 9 0537. Perfection!!!

Serial # 9 0612. A very nice moderately flamed '59 with the pickguard removed showing off what's left of its original cherryburst finish. Photo credit, Val Kolbeck "Guitarville Seattle"

Serial # 9 0605. Some of the bursts in the 9 0600 series have large neck heels. This usually translates to a bigger neck profile. Photo credit, Val Kolbeck "Guitarville Seattle"

Serial # 9 0918. *An absolutely magnificent '59 from the 9 0900 series with strong color and an excellent flamed top. One great looking burst. Photo credit, David Belzer.*

Serial # 9 0653. Photo credit, Charlie Daughtry.

Keith Nelson

"I was very apprehensive about taking my burst on tour. You hear so many   horror stories of damage and theft of instruments, and playing over 200   shows a year puts alot of wear and tear on gear. But then I found myself talking about my guitar more than I was playing it, and that just didn't   seem right, so I made the decision to take it out. I'm so glad I did. I don't know why I didn't do it sooner. It's a little bit of magic every night. These guitars were made to be played."

— Keith Nelson

Photo credit, Chad Mercurio.

Keith Nelson's burst # 9 1062 nicknamed "Louis."

Serial # 9 0597. *A top notch '59 with a superb, perfectly bookmatched flamed maple top which faded to a very attractive honeyburst finish*

Serial # 9 1868. **One of my all time favorite bigsby bursts. I love the look of the irregular wide flame on this beauty. Nicknamed "Cooper." Photo credit, Dave Paetow.**

Serial # 0 2190. Photo credit, Joe Menza.

Serial # 9 3182. This photo shows how this burst looks today. Photo credit, Richard Henry Guitars.

The black and white photo is an image of UK's Mike Dean and The Kinsmen from the early 1960's. The burst in the photo was owned by John Bowen who purchased the guitar from Farmer's Music Store in 1961. At some point it wound up in the hands of Keith Richards. Photo source, The Les Paul Forum.

Serial # 8 6735. Photo credit, Bob Cannon.

Serial # 0 1926. 1960 Gibson Les Paul Standard, serial number 0 1926,
tight shallow flames and a faded 'Iced Tea' color are overshadowed by the circular-
patterned cross-grain of this flat-sawn maple top. Nicknamed 'The All-Seeing Eye'
by its former owner Howard Leese of 'Heart', it appears on many Heart recordings.
Submitted by: Lou Gatanas.

Serial # 0 0210. I got this guitar in 1971. The original owner wanted to buy a color TV set so he sold the 60 LP to get it. Three hundred dollars bought him a nice big console. I've owned and played it ever since. Pat O'Donnell.

No Regrets

My first, and still my favorite one to play. And not because of the neck shape [which I like just fine] but because the sound is the most "articulate" of any of my Bursts. By that, I mean it covers all the bases quite well, from "pretty" to "aggressive". To me, Sandy is a very aggressive sound, but I can't dial it back if the next song is sweet, like Van Morrison's Tupelo Honey.

The story of me buying it in 1975 has been told often. Local store, paid $2,000, I was "the crazy idiot who paid $2000 for a used guitar". Right after I bought it, I drove it down to Houston to show Bart. He worried that I got a fake or conversion, or just a bad one. I walked in on band practice at his house, and he immediately checked it out, and was satisfied I made a great purchase. So was I, and I still am. I have sold many "better" Bursts, but I have never regretted keeping this one. It has never been for sale.

My second Burst was 2 digits off (0-7450), Burly, the only Burst sold at the first Dallas Show in 1978. Curly and Burly...my Burst Brothers. When I bought Curly I was playing a 68GT converted [by Bart] to a Burst.

— Tom Wittrock

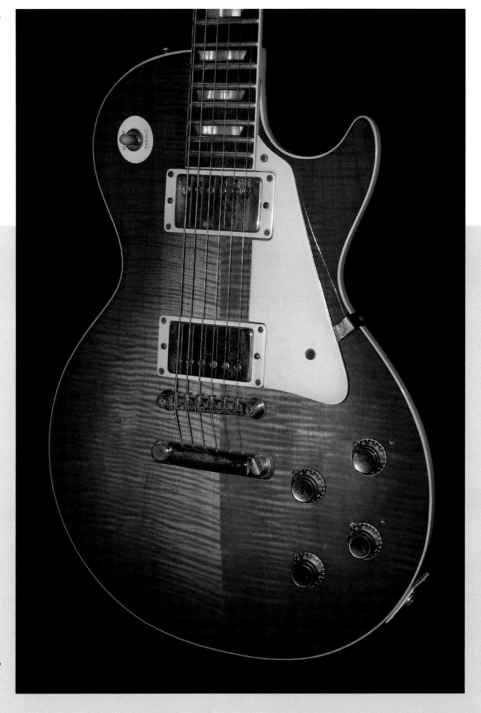

Serial # 0 7448.
Nicknamed "Curly."

Cold Call

The serial number on this one is 9 0645. Jim Anderson found this Burst for me. He made a cold call to a music store and said that he was buying guitars and wanted to know if they had any vintage guitars available for sale. The owner asked him if he was looking for anything specific and Jim told her he was looking for a 1959 Les Paul Standard. She told him that one walked into the store yesterday. What are the odds of that? Jim called me and told me about it and I threw the kids in the car and told him I'd meet him at the store. It was about a 5 hour drive for me. We got there late checked into a hotel and waited till morning. At 9:00 am sharp Jim, my three children and I were standing at the front door waiting for the door to open. About 3 hours later after thoroughly inspecting the guitar, we all walked out of the store with guitar in hand. I actually think I was "bear hugging" it just to make sure the handle or latches didn't break.

— **Daryl (Marty) Schiff**

Serial # 9 0645

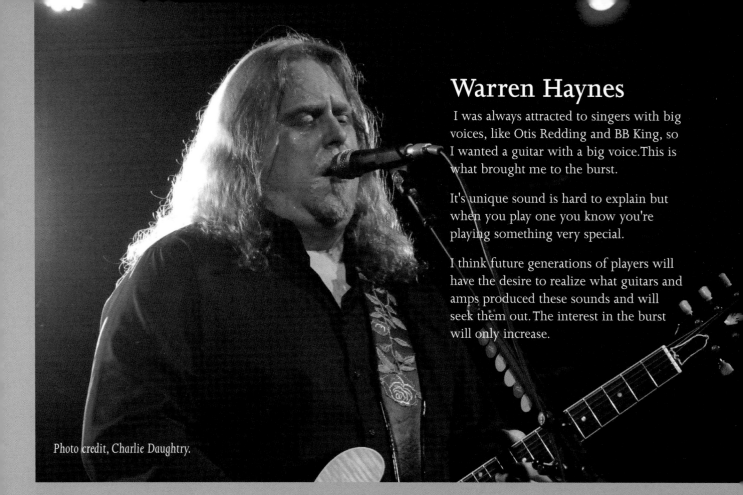

Warren Haynes

I was always attracted to singers with big voices, like Otis Redding and BB King, so I wanted a guitar with a big voice. This is what brought me to the burst.

It's unique sound is hard to explain but when you play one you know you're playing something very special.

I think future generations of players will have the desire to realize what guitars and amps produced these sounds and will seek them out. The interest in the burst will only increase.

Photo credit, Charlie Daughtry.

Serial # 9 1983. Photo credit, Dave Belzer.

Serial # 9 0600. *A superlative burst with a stunning top. Note the original hang tag shadow in the toggle area.*

First Burst By 'Uncle Lou' Gatanas

I suppose my interest in Les Paul guitars began with Jimmy Page, just like everyone else. But my love affair with bursts began in the early 80's when I first laid eyes upon the '59 burst in the JBL speaker ad in Guitar Player Magazine. I was a 'Fender guy' back then because I liked Strats, but mostly, I couldn't afford a Gibson…trips to Manhattan's west 48th street always confirmed that. I'd occasionally see a burst hanging in the window of 'Alex Music' or 'We Buy Guitars' priced around $3,500 (market value at the time). But as far as I was concerned, that was more money than the national debt; I couldn't even afford to dream about owning one!

The years rolled by and I continued dabbling in old Strats, and making the occasional pilgrimage to 'The Block' (west 48th street) just to make myself sick. The year was 1986; I'd already been going to vintage guitar shows and making contacts in the business. One of those contacts was Gil Southworth of Southworth Guitars in D.C. He and I were on the phone weekly discussing his Strat inventory, when in the fall of '86 we mapped out a possible trade deal. He had a '55 two-tone sunburst, Ash body, Bakelite part Strat in good shape, and I had a near-mint three-tone '58 Strat…we agreed to trade straight across. He suggested I fly down there to complete the deal and see his massive inventory so I happily obliged.

This was when things started getting surreal; I flew all the way down to D.C. from NYC, took a cab to his shop, but his '55 Strat wasn't set up…it was unplayable with no strings and no nut! He apologized for his '55 Strat not being set up with words to the effect of "Homina-Homina-Homina", but at least

Photo credit, Lisa Sharken

he liked my '58 Strat. Being somewhat disheartened, I decided to browse his inventory since I was down there anyway. Almost immediately, I noticed a gorgeous two-tone maple neck Strat that turned out to be a '54…the first year of issue and another 'dream guitar' for me. So I went over to him in 'the Gibson room' to ask the price, he said it was $3,000 which was a staggering amount of money for me back then. Still somewhat in a state of sticker shock, I noticed a Les Paul hanging on the wall behind him. I asked him what it was and he nonchalantly said it was a '59…my heart stopped beating. "Are you kidding me…can I take a look at it?" He graciously pulled it down and handed it to me. I couldn't believe my eyes, I actually had an original '59 burst in my hands and it was a nice one with lots of color and tight flame. I was afraid to ask the price, but after playing it a bit, I decided to man-up and find out what it would cost me…my knees buckled when he said the price was $7,000.

At this point, I was outside myself or perhaps just outside my mind; I had no control as to what was coming out of my mouth, like I was a vessel and someone else was speaking through me. So I asked him what the 'package price' of the '54 Strat and the '59 Burst would be. He replied that $9,500 would take them both. I then asked how much my '58 Strat would be worth to him in the deal…he said $2,500. So I thought, "Hmm…I only paid $1,900 for that Strat and he wants to give me $2,500 for it?" The next word that came out of my mouth forever changed my life…"DEAL". He then asked when I could get the balance to him, and I said in about one month…once again, I had no idea what I saying. I suddenly found myself $7,000 in the hole with only one month to dig myself out. Mind you, at the time I had no idea what $7,000 even looked like, nor how to get it in 'any' amount of time, much less in one month!

About a week later, Gil called to find out how I was making out on getting the balance together. When I told him pretty good, he said something came up and he needed me to send him $1,000 immediately, which I did. But as the deadline was approaching, I found myself no closer to the $6,000 balance; I was running out of time & options. Then, 'at the 11th hour', a relative came through for me and loaned me the money I needed to complete the deal. All I can say is the 2nd plane ride back to NYC from D.C. was a lot more enjoyable than the 1st one; I was on my way home with my two dream guitars, and firmly on my way to a new life and my new career!

— Lou Gatanas

Uncle Lou's Classic Guitars, Inc.

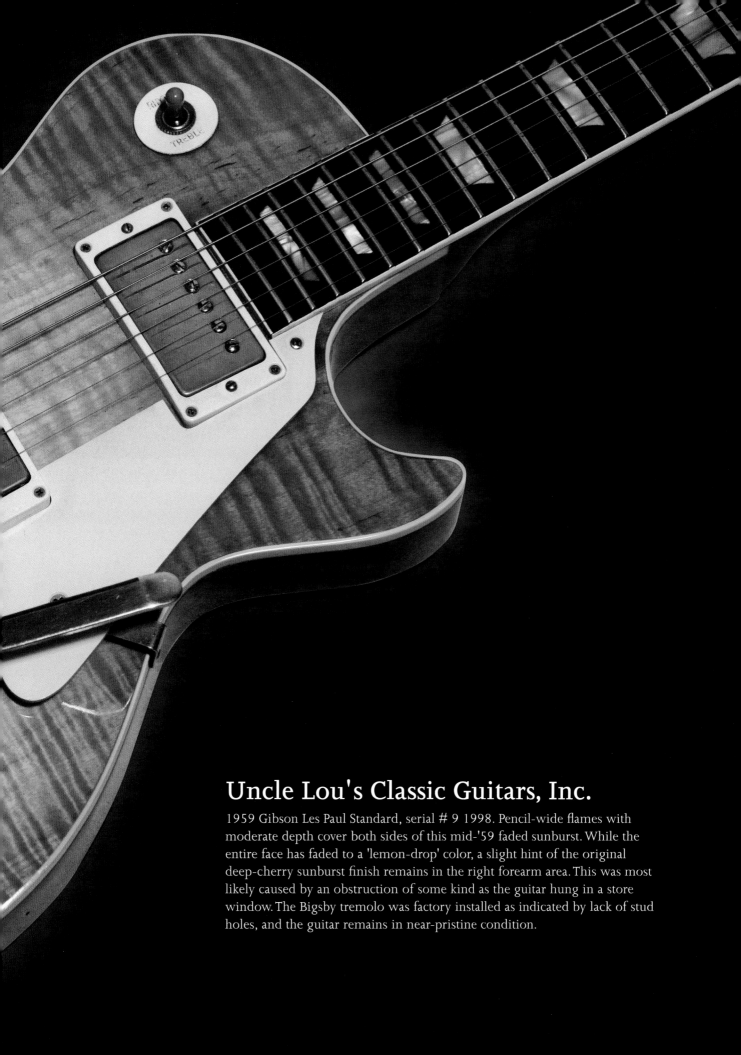

Uncle Lou's Classic Guitars, Inc.

1959 Gibson Les Paul Standard, serial # 9 1998. Pencil-wide flames with moderate depth cover both sides of this mid-'59 faded sunburst. While the entire face has faded to a 'lemon-drop' color, a slight hint of the original deep-cherry sunburst finish remains in the right forearm area. This was most likely caused by an obstruction of some kind as the guitar hung in a store window. The Bigsby tremolo was factory installed as indicated by lack of stud holes, and the guitar remains in near-pristine condition.

Paul Stanley

The Burst will continue to conjure up ongoing decades of defining moments in rock and blues. The sad dilemma though is that as their value continues to soar higher and higher, the actual guitars are heard less and less. The ultimate beauty of the Burst is it's sound and that cannot be heard when they go unused, locked away in a vault. Great art is meant to be seen and great musical instruments are meant to be played. When people buy primarily as an investment they stifle and smother the true purpose of greatness, which is to be experienced, enjoyed and elicit an emotional response. Hoarding for investment purposes denies many the joy of owning one of these magical messengers. Vintage Sunburst Les Pauls aren't stocks or bonds or another addition to a portfolio.

Magic does exist. Let's make sure it doesn't become little more than myth and legend.

— Paul Stanley

Paul's latest acquisition is burst # 9 1225. The burst has been restored by Gordon Miller. The guitar was refinished in the early 70's but the area around the serial number was kept intact. This burst had a 1970's style Gibson cherryburst finish after the first refin but Gordon now gave it a correct era faded burst finish. Photo credit, Gordon Miller.

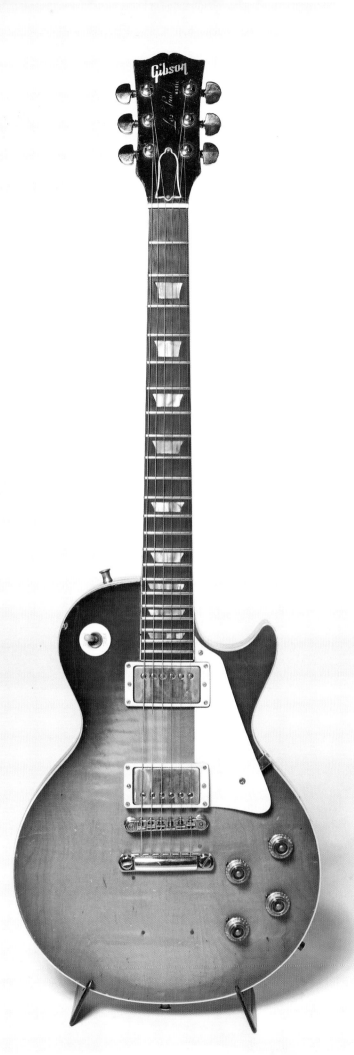

Steve Lukather

"Here is my 1959 Sunburst 9 0494 Les Paul. I bought this in a little store in Arizona in 1979 while on the road. Those were the days when you could still find them. This was my #1 guitar for many years and I used it on the 2nd Toto tour and countless sessions. It is on many hit records of varied styles as well. I am told it has a nick name the ' Rosanna Burst' as I used it on most of the Toto IV record and that song. It was in the video so perhaps thats why. It was on a lot of hit records. A few examples are 'Beat it' by Michael Jackson, 'I love LA 'Randy Newman, 'Runnin with the Night' by Lionel Richie, Quincy Jones 'Baby Come to Me' and 'Just Once' to Olivia Newton John's Lets Get Physical (ok to laugh here but I did the solo haha) I could go on but you get the drift. It is a bit if a magical guitar that make many kinds of sounds and I cherish it. I am afraid to take it anywhere now...hahaha... but I still have it and use it on records and it will be in my family forever."

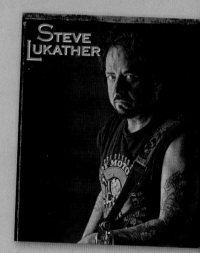

Steve Lukather

Serial # 9 0494. Photo credit, Rick Gould.

Billy Squier with James Cotton and "Fanny". 2011.

Billy Squier

The Burst has become such a prominent part of our musical history, its legacy is all but guaranteed. All the elements are in place: exquisitely-crafted instruments...produced in severely limited quantities...appearing in the hands of rock and blues luminaries for nearly five decades...signature appearances on ground-breaking records (think Bluesbreakers w / Eric Clapton and Led Zeppelin II for starters)...dwindling numbers due to damage and hoarding by wealthy collectors... The Burst is a modern-day Stradivarius, and for those of us fortunate enough to play one (or three), a part of our musical present and future. They are, and will continue to be, truly inspirational instruments.

— Billy Squier

Bridgehampton, NY.

Serial # 0 8098. Photo credit,
Hank's Vintage Guitar Shop.

Serial # 9 1238. *Lazing on a Sunny Afternoon.*

Serial # 9 1950

These two bursts have consecutive serial numbers and both were sold by the Skinner Auction Company. 9 1951 is owned by Joe Bonamassa and is nicknamed "Principal Skinner." Both photos courtesy of Charlie Daughtry.

Serial # 9 1951

Serial # 9 0891. Ed King's longtime sidekick *"Red Eye."*

Special Lady

9 1228, nicknamed "Sandy," has always been a special Burst to me, because I have never seen another top quite like it. The 3-D effect of the curly maple is special, not quite like other flame monsters I have owned [like 9-1981]. Sandy has more notoriety than any of my Bursts, and when Gibson copied it for their Collector's Choice series [CC#4] it pre-sold out! It was so well known and thought of that dealers lined up before production and the entire run was pre-sold! In May of 2012 I let Joe Bonamassa play it at his concert here in Springfield Missouri, and afterwards his comments were very positive. I offered it to him for the rest of his tour and it was seen on many stages across the country [and very well photographed by Charlie Daughtry]. I am sure either I or Charlie has shared those photos, but in case you want one, here is one I like. I still take it out and play it, and it is a real popular piece whenever I take it to Arlington or Dallas for the vintage guitar shows.

Photo Credit, Roxy Kraber.

— Tom Wittrock

1959 Les Paul Standard, serial # 9 1878, formerly owned by *Ace Frehley* of 'KISS'. He used it extensively during his time with KISS and the early days of his solo career. Deep-wide 3-D flames cover the entire face of this guitar and most certainly deserves an 'Uber-Burst' rating...simply mesmerizing! Photo and narration courtesy of Lou Gatanas and Al Romano.

Burst 0 8145 was at one point in its life
owned by a cufflink wearing guitar player
named Johnny B. who wore away the finish
in the area above the pickups. After this
occurred, Johnny B. affixed a celluloid "name
plate" strip to cover the wear.

Dave Thornhill, The Burst That Got Away...

In early 1959, while a senior in High School at Portsmouth East High in Portsmouth Ohio, My Brother John (up-right Bass) and I joined Billy Adams's band the Rock-a-Teers. The band consisted of Billy Adams, vocals and rhythm guitar, Bill's brother Charlie and I on lead guitars, Randal McKenny on Drums, John Thornhhill and Curt May on up-right basses. We were the only rock-a-billy band at that time that featured 2 up-right basses. We recorded several songs at that time, that are still being played on rock-a-billy stations all over the world. For looks, Charlie and I wanted matching guitars for the band for visual effects. We went into a music store

(Reitz Music) in Portsmouth Ohio, and talked with salesman Paul Bramer, and told him what we were looking for. We wanted 2 guitars that were exactly alike. We would have bought any guitar as long as there were 2 of them. Paul showed us guitars hanging on the wall. 2 1958 Les Paul standards that were Cherry/Sunburst in color. We thought the red color in the guitars were a little far out, but since that were the only 2 guitars alike in the store, we bought them anyway. Little did we know at the time what we had just bought. These guitars are on several of Billy's recordings. Our band stayed in tack for about a year and a half. John and I left southern Ohio and moved to the northern part of the state. We met other musicians and formed another band. Meanwhile I was really into Chet Atkins style of playing, so I sold my 58 Burst to my older brother Jr. Thornhill, who was a big influence on me taking up lead guitar, to buy a Gretsch Country Gentleman in order to get the Chet sound. My brother Jr. kept the 58 Burst for a few years and sold it to a man in W. Va. In 1969 I joined Loretta Lynn's band, and 2 months later my brother John joined. By 1973 I began hearing how valuable the 58, 59, and 60 cherry/ sunburst were becoming. I called my brother Jr. and asked him if he knew where my old Les Paul was and if he thought he could get it back for me. He said that he would contact the man he sold it to and find out. He called me back later and said the man stated that he would have to have $600.00 for it. I told my Brother Jr. that if he could get it back for me, that I would buy him any guitar that he wanted with no question asked. He called me back a few days later and said he had my guitar. I asked him what kind of guitar he wanted, and he said he wanted a Gibson 335 red in color with a bigsby tremolo bar. I told him I would get him one. A few days later Loretta Lynn and Conway Twitty were playing a concert in Oklahoma City, Ok. Conway introduced me to Tom Woods, his friend that owned a big music store there. I asked Tom if he had a Gibson 335 Cherry guitar with a Bigsby tail piece, he said he had one. He let me have the guitar for $300.00, and It took it to my brother Jr's house and traded even up for my Old 1958 Les Paul. One mistake I made in 1973, is that I took my 58 to the Gibson factory and asked the quality control person if they would clean the back of the neck for me. The guitar had some nicks in the back of the neck. When I went to the factory in Kalamazoo Mi. I drove Loretta's bus right to the front door. When all the people saw her bus they came out to see what was going on. I was the only one on the bus. However I gave some of the managers, photos, albums, tee shirts. posters of Loretta, so I was OK with them. The mistake was the factory refinished the entire guitar and restored it like new, which was great at the time, but it dropped the value of the guitar by 50%. I kept the guitar until about 5years ago. George Gruhn of Gruhns Guitar in Nashville sold the guitar for me. The guitar brought six figures plus a few thousand. But Mr. Gruhn said it would have brought double that if the guitar hadn't been re-finished. My advice to anyone who has a vintage instrument is, don't mess with the instrument what so ever.

— **Dave Thornhill**

Serial # 8 5388. Nicknamed "The Other Woman." Photo credit, Tom Wittrock.

Serial # 8 5397. There's something about the cherry sunburst on a 1958 Les Paul. When unfaded, it's one of the prettiest finishes on a burst. Photo credit, Richard Henry Guitars.

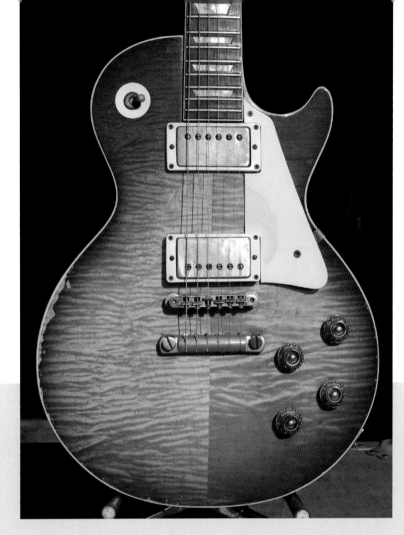

Serial # 9 1171. A nice close up of "Pearly." Photo credit, Pat Foley, Gibson Custom Shop.

The "Reverend" Billy Gibbons surrounded by a flock of "Pearly" Les Paul reissues. Also pictured are Pat Foley (left) and Edwin Wilson (right) from Gibson's Custom Shop.

Charlie Daniels

Losing a vintage Les Paul Sunburst that you've spent so many years of your life with is almost like losing an old friend. You could try 1000 others and never find another guitar that had your personal "feel" built into it.

— *Charlie Daniels*

Here's a photo of Charlie's stolen 1958 burst.

Shrunken tuner tips are quite a common occurrence on many bursts. A few more tunings on tips like these and they will likely crumble in your hand

Serial # 9 1242.

Serial # 9 0945. A pristine '59 burst recently surfaced from the original owner's family and was sold by Elderly Instruments in Michigan. This burst has all its original color remaining!

A New Home

I was in my early 20's when I sold 9 1688. The guitar was my favorite of the 15 or so 58-60 bursts we had in stock. She was lightweight, had just the right kind of flame and the color, at the time, was a very light Tea Burst. It had a double white (or cream for you purists) in the neck and a black in the back. The sustain was really pretty remarkable. I didn't have a lot of "hands on" experience with Standards at the time, but this guitar really spoke to me. She was one of the first , if not the first that I sold to Ronnie Proler. I don't think the price was more than $4500, but it may have been a little less (you can check with Proler)

After that guitar, there were many, that passed through the shop and my hands. But I always remembered her. For some reason she just stuck with me.

Fast forward 30+ years and I was invited to visit with Joe Bonamassa for his sound check at the Hard Rock in Hollywood Fl. Mike, guitar tech extraordinaire, greeted me and immediately started showing me Joe's "road gear". Then he whips out "Spot" from it's 70's Protector case and I say "Mike, I know this guitar." He handed it to me and it just hit me like a ton of bricks. This guitar felt just like it did to me all those years ago. I've been selling vintage guitars for almost 40 years and that never happens.

Spot has surely found her "forever home" with Joe and watching him play it and hearing it at it's full potential the little sadness and sense of loss melted from me in the notes and I knew the guitar was happier with him than she would ever be with me. If you ever have the opportunity to see Joe and Spot do their dance, get over there and feel the love he has for her and she for him.

Narration by Timm Kummer.

Serial # 9 1688. Photo credit, Mike Hickey.

Serial # 9 1918. 1959 Burst.

Collectors Choice

I first became attracted to Les Pauls as a teenager, in my first band named "Cold Sweat." Our lead guitar player, Bill, had a 1957 Goldtop with humbuckers and a Marshall Stack! He was an awesome guitarist, and was a tall, handsome dude with flowing blonde hair and a real ladies' man – the epitome of a rock musician! His Les Paul was always on my mind until I purchased my first Les Paul Reissue in 1993. It took a few years, but my interest to acquire a Burst was heightened after reading Vic DaPra's first book, 'Burst, which was first published in 1994. So thanks, Vic, for getting me hooked! My 1959 Burst was the first one I purchased. I was blown away by its pristine condition and its beautiful unfaded Cherryburst color. If you look closely, there is a shadow tag on the body to the left of the tailpiece. It is very clean, with minimal checking and dings. This guitar weighs in the mid 8 pound range and has a beautiful , bright sounding bridge pickup. This Burst was selected by Gibson's Custom Shop for their Collector's Choice series, as CC#6. Edwin Wilson from Gibson Custom flew to my home and spent a few days measuring and photographing the guitar, and he digitally scanned the neck for sizing. I think they did a great job of matching the color and vibe of this Burst with the Collector's Choice version.

— Mike Stubowski

Serial # 9 1854. Here's a larger look at this super burst nicknamed "Ouch."

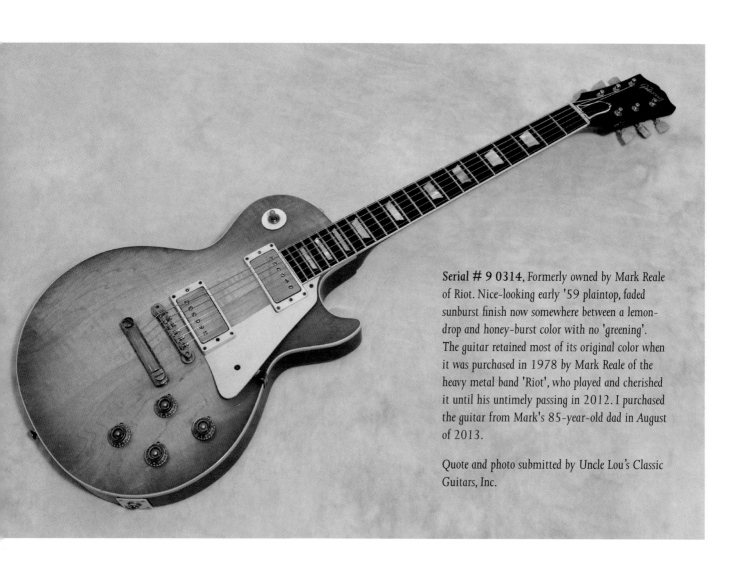

Serial # 9 0314, Formerly owned by Mark Reale of Riot. Nice-looking early '59 plaintop, faded sunburst finish now somewhere between a lemon-drop and honey-burst color with no 'greening'. The guitar retained most of its original color when it was purchased in 1978 by Mark Reale of the heavy metal band 'Riot', who played and cherished it until his untimely passing in 2012. I purchased the guitar from Mark's 85-year-old dad in August of 2013.

Quote and photo submitted by Uncle Lou's Classic Guitars, Inc.

Serial # 9 1908. Known in the 'burst community as the NBT (next best thing) '59. This guitar was sold by Norm's Rare Guitars in the mid 1980's. There is a cardboard figure made to size of this burst and was sold as the NBT '59. Photo credit, The Vintage Guitar Boutique UK.

Serial # 8 6756. Photo credit, Rick Phipps.

Greg Martin

It's the wee hours of the morning as I write this rolling down the road on a tour bus, I'm on the way home after a 3 day run with The Kentucky HeadHunters. I've been on the road playing music for over 36 years now, what an amazing journey it's been. Has much changed since I hit the road in 1977? In the 70's I had a dream that one day I would make a living playing Guitar, and by the Grace of God, I have done that very thing. I quit my day job in 1977, and I've never looked back or regretted where music has taken me in my life. I have been fortunate to do what I love, and I still love what I do. Another big part of my dream as a teenager was to one day own a 1958 sunburst Les Paul Standard, and thanks to Hank Williams Jr, that dream came true in 1990. The moment that I plugged the 1958 Les Paul into a vintage Marshall, my quest for tone was over. Some of you know that John Sebastian planted the seed for me. When I first saw John Sebastian play his 1959 Les Paul Standard with The Lovin' Spoonful in 1966, I became infatuated with the instrument. Two years later I heard Michael Bloomfield with The Electric Flag and on the "Super Session" and "Live Adventures" albums, my fate was sealed. Seeing Jimmy Page, Peter Green, Mick Taylor, Billy F. Gibbons, Ronnie Montrose, Joe Walsh, Paul Kossoff, Duane Allman, Dickey Betts, Jeff Beck, Phil Keaggy, Eric Clapton and others in the 70's play 50's Les Paul's 'bursts put me on the very path that I'm on today. There's nothing more musical to my ears than plugging my 1958 into an old Marshall or 50's tweed Fender amp, the Guitar helped me find my own musical voice. Every 50's Les Paul 'burst has it's own unique tone, and I'm absolutely in love with the way my 1958 sounds, plays and looks. The Gibson Custom Shop is

Photo credit, Rick Phipps.

now building "Collector's Choice #15," a Les Paul patterned after my very own 1958. How cool is that?! For a guy that grew up in a small town with big aspirations, I've realized many of my dreams. I've won a Grammy, American Music, CMA and ACM Awards, I have Gold and Platinum Records, but getting the 1958 Les Paul is my greatest accomplishment as a musician. I thank God every day for my Les Paul, and I'm forever indebted to Hank Williams Jr. for bestowing the 1958 on me in 1990. I could care less about the market values. Even if the Les Paul market crashed tomorrow, I'd still cherish my 1958, it's a big part of me. It's traveled many miles with me, it's on the majority records I've made since 1990, the joy from playing the guitar transcends any monetary value, God willing, I will play the 1958 the rest of my life. God gives each one of us a Guitar or two, I've been lucky to find mine. And yes, my 1958 is here on the bus with me tonight, I'm looking at it as I write this. May God bless each and every one of you in your musical journey, and may you find that very instrument that inspires and pushes you to realize your musical dreams.

— Greg Martin

Serial # 9 2340. *Photo credit, Charlie Daughtry.*

The Monumentally Misunderstood PAF

My background is in graphic design, art direction, illustration, 35 years worth. Much of my career was focused in the music industry, I had EMG Pickups and Shrapnel Records as clients and helped both of them establish professional images in published print media for 14 and 25 years respectively, and have done hundreds of album art packages for many famous guitar players. For the last 13 years I have been a full time guitar pickup designer, delving deep into the craft and science of how pickups work, using obsessive study and experimentation. My main "love affair" has been with original vintage Gibson PAF humbuckers, a subject that the more I learned how they do what they do, the more I realized almost no one really knows them very well, and many myths and mistaken ideas abound on that subject.

PAF's were Seth Lover's idea, though his original Patented design was a double slug coil pickup with no pole screws: Gibson forced him to add adjustable screws like their P90's had, because it was a "sales" feature. He did not invent humbuckers, in fact Gibson hired him to make something similar to Gretsch's preceding humbucking product. Among the things he has said publicly, were "we wound them until they were full--we wound them to inductance--we wound them to 5,000 turns." Also, that "we used soft iron." The truth is that the PAF magnetic circuit used 3 different alloys of steel, each contributing part of its total voice with the slug poles, adjustable screw poles and pole keeper. Seth only used the "soft iron" that was available in Gibson's stock room, and had no idea what those materials actually were. Vintage steel is not the same as modern steel, the pole keeper for instance, used an alloy impossible to find from any modern supplier, vintage steel was made by old open hearth Bessemer steel plants and can't be copied 100%. Even the other 2 groups of poles are made of steel with no exact modern equivalent.

The magnet wire used was not pure copper as it is today, the insulation recipe is not the same as we have now, the old wire sounds different, for quite a few reasons that I have, detailed in lab print-outs, from the industry leader in magnet wire manufacturing today, who examined quite a few samples of vintage plain enamel wire I have saved over the years. The coils were wound to one winding pattern with a certain number of turns per layer. There is a mistaken idea the the two coils were wound different amounts, which is somewhat generally true, but the bobbins (made of butyrate plastic) were not identical designs, so 5,000 winds on each bobbin would give you different readings anyway. In my experiments, using different mismatches in turns on each coil did not offer up any noticeable "magic," as most people think, and there is no secret to PAF tones in that mismatch. There is also a rather stellarly ignorant idea out there, promoted by a few, that a vintage coil winding machine can produce "PAF tone." This is an absurd idea and holds no water. Any machine auto winder can be made to wind a PAF correct coil as long as the operator is educated and experienced; the coils are not the secret to PAF tone anyway. There IS no ONE secret.

Vintage magnets, were also radically different, they offer up a very dry and very bright sound, but stay inches below being shrill. I've been sent quite a few attempts at copying them but no one has succeeded. Vintage technologies and materials are just not possible to replicate.

These old magnets don't sound so great in modern pickups, they worked best in the darker vintage magnet wire coils.

So few guitar players have ever played a working vintage PAF, they don't know them when they hear them. They reference classic rock recordings, and think that those buckers were very warm and fat sounding, many commercial pickup companies exploit that idea. The truth though, is those recordings are an engineer's sonic artwork and don't represent what you will experience if you sat down with a vintage Les Paul in your bedroom. You would surprised to find the pickups are quite bright, but with that brightness comes a

harmonically rich and fat vocal sound thats impossible to describe, touch sensitivity, and a dynamic quality of being able to whisper and immediatley break out into a fearsome screaming solo, a great dynamic range full of SOUL.

Books on vintage Les Pauls seldom say anything useful about old PAF's, probably because most know little about them. In my study I found they had a wide range of how much wire, and different diameters of wire on them, with a wide range of DC resistance readings. There is no way to date any of them to any particular year, except that the short magnets showed up around late '59 and onwards. The earlier long magnets were all very rough sand cast, the short magnet began to be ground to a certain thickness, giving a polished look. Earlier PAF's had double black coils leads, in '61 they began changing to black and white.

PAF's can be authenticated by the decals and paper tape, both which glow greenish under black light, both impossible to fake. Most PAF's read around 7.5K, because the recipe of 5,000 winds per coil gives you that result. 10,000 turns total recipe was borrowed directly from Gibson's P90's. Classic rock heroes, though, did not like these recipe pickups and opted for the stronger output ones in the 8-9K ranges, because their amps were not master volume and most did not use boost pedals; a hotter pickup is what did the trick. I think it was no coincidence that our rock heroes preferred the later short magnet PAF's as these generally had better power and clarity than earlier years.

Another neglected area on the subject of PAF equipped LP's, is the wiring harness. At least 40% of the tone is in the harness. Vintage braided shield wire doesn't age very well and some "bad" sounding old 'bursts may only have degraded wire, worn out pots and caps. The harness wire is a huge "tone cap" in itself, modern braided shield wire is noticeably different as well. Vintage pots used in Gibson's guitars were all over the map, ranging from about 400k up to 650K and even higher values. These can also have a big effect on how a vintage axe sounds. The best tone caps were the paper in oil Sprague "bees." Not all bees were paper in oil, you can tell by the filler cap on one end that its an oil filled capacitor. The other bees were some kind of mylar and not as desirable. Cap values also varied but not as much as pot values. Caps ranged from .020uf up to .034uf. The actual physical way the harness was wired, its exact circuit is a big part of vintage Les Paul tone, so much so

that anything I sell, I make sure its going into a correctly constructed replica 50's harness, this is KEY.

As an investment, a vintage PAF can be a crap shoot. Its best to buy one thats never had its cover off. The cover protects the coils from human sweat, which is an acid/salt mixture that only a drop or two getting in through the circle/square hole will eat the wire; every single PAF I have restored died with its cover off. I had one recently where sweat ate thru the entire end of the coil under the little top hole, pretty ugly. I cringe when I see a vintage Les Paul being played with uncovered PAF's, its a real bad idea.

My own personal work in replicating vintage PAF's was extremely long and complex work, involved several industry experts who helped me for free, it took a long time to truly understand exactly how and WHY they sound the way they do. Having a thick folder of lab data does not tell anyone how to make those pickups, the work I did was interpretive and intuitive, with thousands of hours of experimentation, lots of money down a hole, and years of prototypes. Many trade secrets came out of my work. The truth is they cannot be 100% copied due to old technologies just having vanished, but I was able to get amazingly close. Close enough that a few customers who own vintage PAF"s sold them and use mine in their place. They are a complex puzzle, each piece matters, each piece must perform correctly or the end results don't appear. They surely do not reveal themselves easily, the old materials have to be studied, one must have a good solid base in the craft of pickup DESIGN to even begin to understand whats going on. There are also no commercial parts you can buy that will help you, I machine all the critical parts myself, the old fashioned slow way. In the end many of my break-through's were total intuitive flashes while spending hours dissecting them on my work bench, and reading through the piles of lab data pages. And too, I made many big mistakes and hit many dead-ends along the way....

My beloved PAF's, a journey that is finally over, coming down a long damn hard road to get the results I did. I do LOVE that sound...

— Dave Stephens

The views expressed in this article are Dave Stephens personal thoughts.

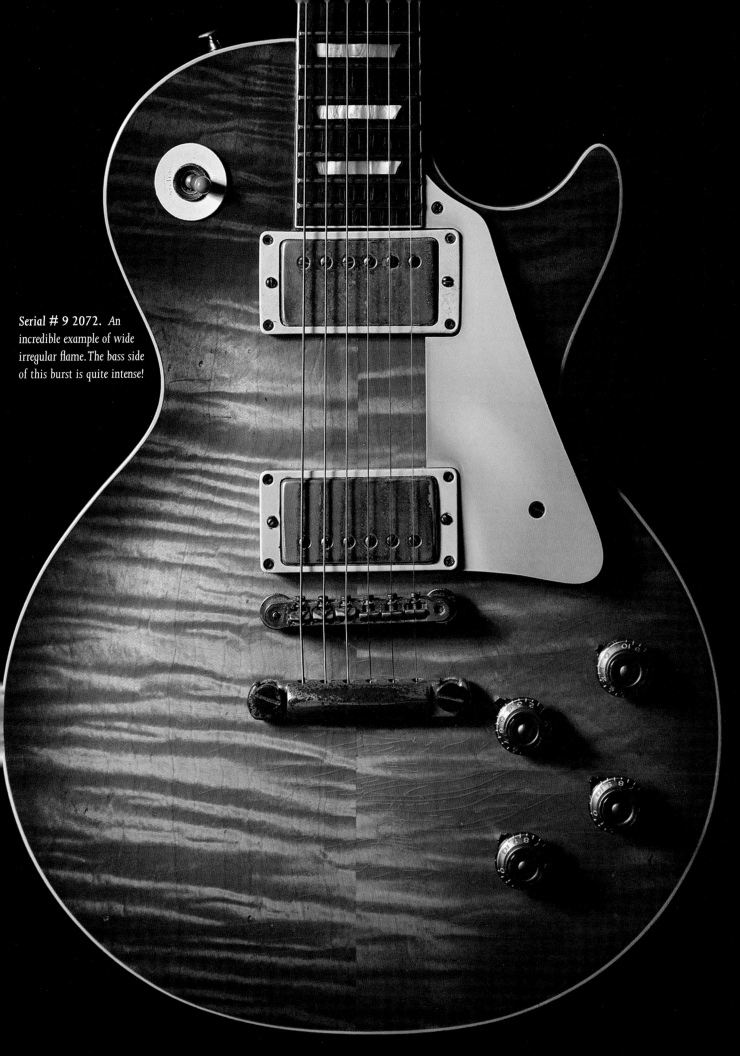

Serial # 9 2072. An incredible example of wide irregular flame. The bass side of this burst is quite intense!

Jimmy Page in the studio during the early days of Led Zeppelin with his #1 burst.

A rare photo of Jimmy Page's #2 burst # 9 1703, Photo credit, Pat Foley, Gibson Custom Shop.

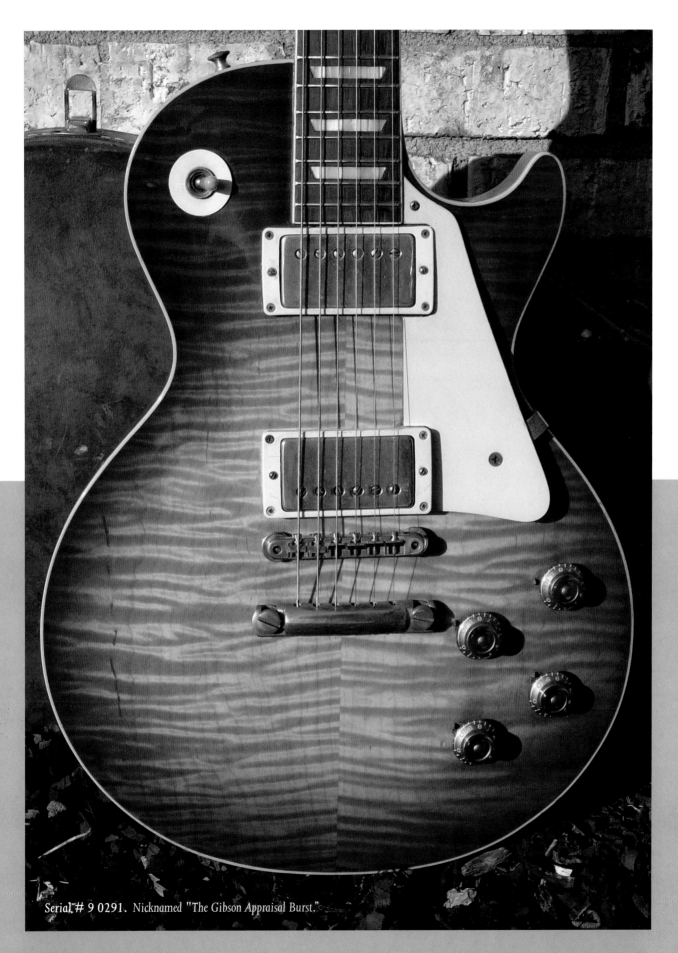

Serial. # 9 0291. Nicknamed "The Gibson Appraisal Burst."

Paul Warren

When I was 14, in 1968, an older musician, who was my mentor, told me
Eric Clapton played an older Les Paul, and they were better than the new
ones. I set about trying to get one. A friend at school , told me his father had
a used Les Paul for sale. I was playing a $50.00 Decca arch top, at the time. I
spoke to my Dad, explained the situation, and he responded that a carpenter
needed the proper tools. We we very poor, so he gave me $100.00, and drove
me there. He said a man should do his own business, and waited in the car.
That was the first time I saw a brown case! When my friends father opened it,
there were only two strings, and it was filthy. It was a 57 Gold Top, with P90s.
Not knowing the difference, I knew I had found the Holy Grail. I negotiated
him down, from $150.00, and walked out, brown case in hand. It was a great
guitar, and I played mostly Gold Tops, with P90s, from that point on. Until
I played a burst. Fast forward to 1973. By this time, there was Led Zepplin,
Jeff Beck was playing a burst, and the Allmans had come out. I had to get a
burst, and it had to have flames! I was playing a club, and a friend dropped
by, after his gig. He had his 60 with him, and he let me play a set with it. The
heavens opened, and the Angels sang. I could play anything I could think of,
and hold notes forever. I was playing through a 59 Bassman, tied up with a 59
Bandmaster, and the combination was mind boggling.
At the time, I had a Gold Top, and a Reverse Firebird
5. I tried to trade both for his burst, but he wasn't
having it. He still has that guitar today. Smart man.
This began my quest. I've since had three 59s, and
one 60, the 60 being the best sounding of the lot,
and it was completely flamed. It's in Robb Lawrence's
first Les Paul book, and there was a large article about it
in Vintage guitar. It belonged to Peter Green for a while, after
me. The purchase of that guitar, and it's subsequent history, is a long story
in itself. Unfortunately, due to the exorbitant cost of a burst, I've not owned
one for some time. I sold my last one to buy my first house, back in the 90s. I
am currently making due with a 1959 ES 335, which is incredible, but I will
always cherish those early days, scanning the paper on Sundays, and asking
around. Looking at pictures, and drooling(I still do). Looking for "used" Les
Pauls, and being willing to pay over $1000.00, for the right burst. If only.

— Paul Warren

Howard Leese at a recent Bad Company concert playing the Clapton / Kossoff / Rodgers 1958 Les Paul. Photo credit, Carl Dunn.

Howard Leese

As of this writing, I am beginning my 17th year playing guitar for the Paul Rodgers Band. Since 2008, I have also had the privilege to tour with Simon Kirke and Mick Ralphs in Bad Company. This summer, we did a two month run with Lynyrd Skynyrd, both bands celebrating their 40th anniversaries. When the tour started, Mick and I decided to see how many Sunburst Les Pauls we could check out. By the time we got to Woodstock for our last show with Skynyrd, we had played 12 Bursts. But on this night, something special happened. The gentlemen who now owns one of Paul Kossoff's old Les Pauls came to the show, and brought the guitar for a visit. This is #8-2453, the guitar that Kossoff got from Eric Clapton in a trade for a Black Beauty Les Paul Custom that Clapton later used on many Cream tracks. It is thought to be the "All Right Now" guitar. The guitar then went to Paul Rodgers, who kept it for many years. A few years ago, Paul auctioned the guitar off, and donated the proceeds to a charity run by David Kossoff, Paul's father. He basically gave the guitar away. The guy who got it from Paul still has it. Before the show, as we were checking it out and taking photos with it, he asked me "would you like to play it tonight?" I replied "absolutely!" I played it for the whole set, and it sounded like thunder, played very easily, and never needed tuning. It is in beautiful condition, not very faded, and for a '58, the neck is not that fat, more like a '59 shape. It was a thrill and an honor to wield this incredible weapon, and a night I will not soon forget.

— **Howard Leese**

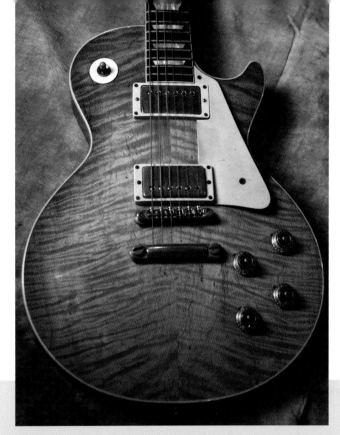

The Outlaws were an early '60's UK instrumental band. Note two things in the photo, the burst on the left hand side in the photo and a very early photo of Ritchie Blackmore in his pre Deep Purple days.

Serial # 9 0799. This burst was originally sold at Guitar Trader in Red Bank, New Jersey to Brad Whitford from Aerosmith. This beauty now resides in the Mike Reeder Collection.

One of Paul Kossoff's main squeeze bursts during the "Free" years. Gibson did a reissue of this guitar in their Custom Shop Signature Series. Photo credit, Pat Foley.

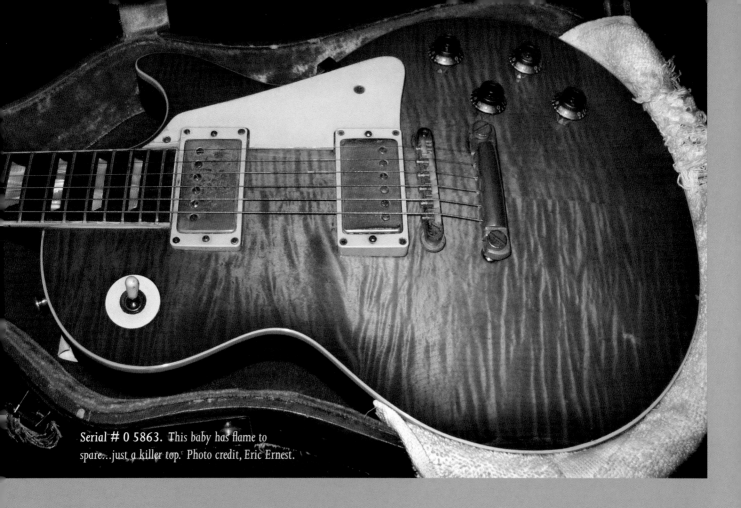

Serial # 0 5863. This baby has flame to
spare...just a killer top. Photo credit, Eric Ernest.

Billy Squier and Joe Bonamassa comparing
bursts backstage. Photo credit, Mike Hickey.

Serial # 9 0633. This guitar has on of the largest necks I've ever felt on a burst...A real handful of pleasure.

Serial # 9 2077. An old school looking '59 showing signs of an added and removed tailpiece at one time. This guitar first surfaced at Guitar Trader in the early 1980's. One fabulous burst in my opinion.

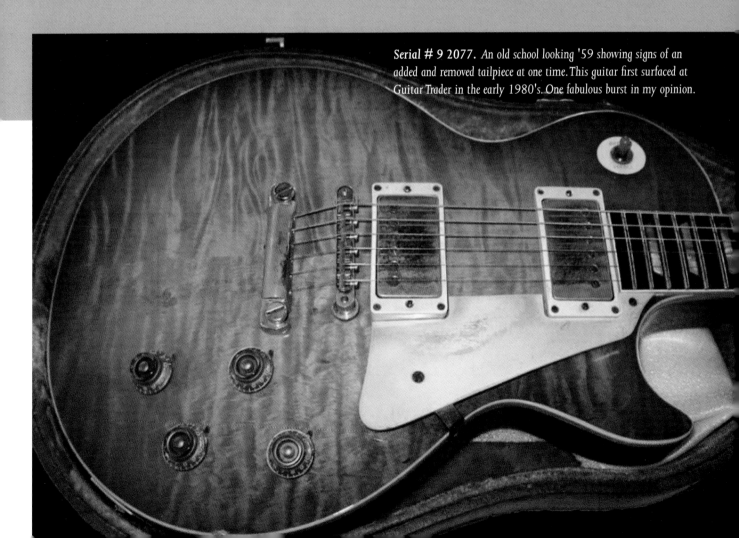

Serial # 0 7590. Here's Joe Walsh's once owned "Rocky Mountain Way" burst. Photo credit, Pat Foley, Gibson Custom Shop.

Back stage photo of Paul McCartney's Big 3 rack. In the middle is Paul's 1960 burst # 0 1182. Photo credit, Pat Foley.

Just listen for a minute...
The sustain... listen to it...You could go and
have a bite an' you'd still be hearin' that one.

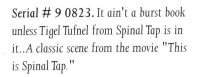

Serial # 9 0823. It ain't a burst book unless Tigel Tufnel from *Spinal Tap* is in it..*A classic scene from the movie "This is Spinal Tap."*

Serial # 0 1485. In this serial number range of bursts the neck starts to become smaller but sunburst finish is more like a '59 and some features such as the knobs and tuners remain unchanged. until mid 1960. This beauty is from the Mike Reeder collection.

Serial # 0 2171. Big flames and double white PAF's...a hard combination to beat. Guitar courtesy Mike Reeder.

Serial # 9 1378

Here's a photo of Aerosmith's Joe Perry and Pat Foley from Gibson's Custom Shop. In the background are a herd of '59 Joe Perry Les Paul Signature models. The reissues are a copy of the famous Joe / Slash burst 9 0663. All Joe Perry photos courtesy of Pat Foley, Gibson Custom Shop.

Serial # 9 2012. *A late '59 which hailed from Salt Lake City. Strong wide flames cover the face of this beautiful honey amber burst.*

Daryl Marty Schiff

A good friend of mine, Matt Scannell of Vertical Horizon, was in town and I wanted to give him a tour of Blackbird Studio and show him our guitar vault. I called another friend of mine, Brett Beavers, to come down and take a look also. We got to the vault and the first two guitars that I wanted to show them were the 1959 and 1960 Bursts. I got them both out and held them up. Matt told me that I should take a picture holding both of them. I didn't bring my camera and the phone that I had at the time didn't take pictures. So Brett told me that he would take the picture on his phone and email it to me. So he did and when I got the email the subject line read "One MEEEEELYUN $ Picture".

— Daryl (Marty) Schiff
DAMM Vintage Guitars

178

Serial # 9 1879. An incredibly wild flamed '59 nicknamed "Harry" after the original owner's first name. Check out the pic of Harry playing this burst. In the original photo, dated April 1960, the cherry sunburst finish was unfaded at the time.

179

Serial # 9 0598. This burst has some great provenance. The guitar was sold at an estate sale in Pennsylvania. There were buyers from across the country placing their bids to get this beauty. The original strap, hang tags and strings are still with the guitar today. It now resides with Brian Ray, member of The Paul McCartney Band and his new band project The Bayonets. One of the cleanest bursts ' on the planet.

Serial # 9 1843. *A pristine*
all original bigsby burst

Serial # 0 0200. Photo credit, Gary Winterflood.

Serial # 8 6743

Waddy Wachtel

My first Les Paul was what they call the "TV" model, yellow double cut away. I had seen a black 3 pickup one when I was 10 years old, I thought I was going to lose my mind, most amazing thing I had ever seen, had to have one. At 11, the tv model became mine. Loved it, but it didn't look like that black one, and then the beatles appeared and I had to have a Gretsch Country Gentleman (why? ha!!), and then came the time to move to California so I gave my little TV model to Leslie West. Got my '60 sunburst from Steve Stills in 1968. Best $350 I ever spent!! World's finest guitar, purest sound, incredible tone, intonation exceptional, perfect neck, which of course I've broken more than once. When I started doing studio work in Los Angeles that was the only electric guitar I had. I used it on countless recordings.

Photo credit, Robert Bruns.

— Waddy Watchel

I would like to thank Kim LaFleur from Historic Makeovers for these photos of Keith Richards burst used during the early 70's with The Stones. It's hard to read the first digit of the serial number in the photo. It's either 8 1217 which is a little early to be a burst or 9 1217 which would make more sense.

Serial # 8 5813. One of my all time favorite burst photos.
This photo pefectly shows the wear and lacquer checking on
the face of this guitar. This burst just oozes with coolness.
Photo credit, Eric Ernest.

Matthias Jabs

Even though I play mostly flashy Explorers or
Stratocasters on stage with the Scorpions, I always
loved Les Pauls and used them quite a lot in the
studio throughout the 35 year career with the band.
In the early eighties I used to own a `58 and a `60
Burst but unfortunately sold them. In recent years I
have been looking for a great Burst from `59 an was
very lucky to find an exceptional guitar in terms of
sound, looks and originality. I am in love with my
"Bigsby Burst" and the ser. nr. is 9 0890 which is
like the area code of Munich (089), where my guitar
store MJ Guitars happens to be Rock`n Roll forever,

— Matthias Jabs

Randy Bachman

I got this guitar in 1967 in Nanaimo, B.C. Canada. I was with The Guess Who before the hits came and playing a church basement. I was playing a turquoise sparkle Mosrite at the time. In the middle of the first song, a young kid walked into the dance with a small brown case. Every guitar player knows this small brown case. He came to the foot of the stage (which was only a foot high), opened the case and pointed at the Gibson LP and then at the Mosrite (a spare gtr and not my regular axe) and motioned if I wanted to play it. So in the middle of the song I switched guitars. I played it all night. At the end of the gig, we formally met, shook hands and I gave him back the Les Paul and thanked him for letting me play it. "You mean you don't want it?" he said. I asked what he was talking about and he said, when I first came in I asked if I wanted to trade guitars and you did! I explained that I didn't hear what he said but I'd love to trade guitars. I told him the Mosrite was not a fair trade and that I'd also give him all the money I had in my pocket as well, which was about $76.00. I asked the minister who was chaperoning the church youth dance to get a piece

of paper with Church letterhead and document and witness the Bill of Sale which he did. Little did I know at the time what that particular Les Paul would mean to me. It would go on to become my signature guitar sound for The Guess Who in hits like "No Time" and "American Woman" but also help shape the sound of Bachman-Turner Overdrive. After many years of playing it on stage, I developed a back problem so I only played it in the studio and left it at home most of the time. Except for a bad buckle rash in the back, it is in amazing pristine condition. In the late 60's -early 70's, I had many conversations with Frank Zappa, Jimmy Page, Alvin Lee, and others who wanted to buy the guitar but I felt very attached to it and am glad I kept it.

Today it lives in the Rock + Roll Hall of Fame in Cleveland and you can add many zeros onto the original price I paid for it.

— *Randy Bachman*

Serial # 9 0614. This burst was once owned by Gary Richrath of REO Speedwagon. Photo credit, Vintage Guitar Boutique UK.

My Rick Derringer story

I BUY A 1959 SUNBURST LES PAUL by Binky Philips

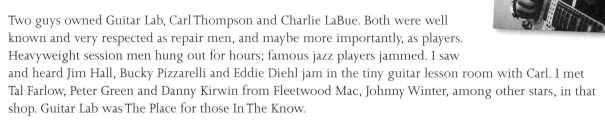

It was the beginning of the Summer of 1970, and I was just back from my first ever trip to London.

I'd caught the Gibson SG Special Pete had thrown to me at the Metropolitan Opera House about four weeks earlier on June 7th. It was missing its headstock and a very hip repair/modification shop, Guitar Lab, had attached another one onto the guitar, a very tricky job, and one that usually fails. Your guitar's head breaks off, it's now a "parts car," nomesane. But, Guitar Lab had made it work. I was broke, so in exchange for building and attaching a headstock to the Gibson Pete had thrown me, it was agreed that I'd 'gopher' for Guitar Lab for the summer. I showed up every morning and got everyone coffee, cigarettes, lunch, changed guitar strings, rang up sales, ran various errands, cleaned up. Eventually, they even wound up paying me.

Two guys owned Guitar Lab, Carl Thompson and Charlie LaBue. Both were well known and very respected as repair men, and maybe more importantly, as players. Heavyweight session men hung out for hours; famous jazz players jammed. I saw and heard Jim Hall, Bucky Pizzarelli and Eddie Diehl jam in the tiny guitar lesson room with Carl. I met Tal Farlow, Peter Green and Danny Kirwin from Fleetwood Mac, Johnny Winter, among other stars, in that shop. Guitar Lab was The Place for those In The Know.

One afternoon later that summer, Teddy Slatus, Edgar Winter's road manager, came in with both of regular-customer Rick Derringer's sunburst Les Pauls. Back in those days, years before reissues, that meant two of maybe 900 total Gibsons made between mid-1958 through the end of 1960 with that glorious fade-from-a-red-to-gold transparent lacquer finish over highly figured maple and the then new and powerful (Patent-Applied-For) Humbucker pickups.

Stars of Rock Guitar, Keith Richards, ylor, Michael Bloomfield, Eric Clapton, Jimmy Page, Duane Allman, and several other major cats had settled on this model Gibson as The One. And to this day, it rightly remains exalted. I had seen only one in person once before, a year earlier, in the window of Jimmy's, one of the coolest of the nine or ten music stores on West 48th St. back in the 1960s. Dazzled, I walked in and asked how much it was. The salesman sneered "$500, and no, you can't play it, kid." I gasped. $500!! That was a psychotically high price for anything smaller than a Chevrolet!

So, now here I was, the gopher/odd job kid at Guitar Lab, and I've been told to take the strings off of both of Ricky's Les Pauls. Oh my! I was gonna get to actually hold these electric Stradivariuses! One Ricky had just bought, and was now his favorite, a very clean cherry Life-Saver red sunburst 1959. The other was a relatively beat up 1959. It was an unusual dark molasses red-brown sunburst. I'd seen photos of various rock stars with their Les Pauls that indicated there were about 4 or 5 shades of cherry and orange sunbursts on these guitars, but, this dark elegant jazz-guitar-style Les Paul was unique and unexpectedly compelling.

Early on in my guitar obsession, in the Spring of 1969, I saw Buddy Guy open for The Who at the Fillmore East. I dug how torn up Buddy's original 50's sunburst Fender Stratocaster was and how fucking cool and "authentic" a guitar looked when it was sorta trashed. From that point on, I always actively sought out beat-up used guitars. Not only were they always cheaper, they always played and sounded better than the mint ones, anyway. The dark Les Paul of Rick's was the exact right kind of beat up. The sides and back were belt-worn and chipped to hell, but, the sunburst face of the guitar was in almost A+ condition. I was utterly thrilled to even be in the same room with these guitars.

While I was handling the dark one, before I removed the strings for the repair, I had an impulse, an urge I didn't even try to resist. I did something naughty. In the lobby of Guitar Lab's building, there was a large 6x10 foot tall mirror by the elevator door. This mirror was only one flight down from Guitar Lab. I don't recall how I was able to get it out and back, but, at some point during that day, I snuck downstairs with the dark Les Paul and took a look at myself, for the first time in my life, holding an actual 1959 sunburst Les Paul. I gave myself about 60 seconds of staring ecstasy before sneaking the guitar back upstairs and into the work area.

A few minutes later, hotheaded Bruce, the guy who was going to do the actual repairs, told me that I needed to copy down the serial number of the dark Les Paul because there was a small hairline crack on the headstock that needed gluing and the serial number was probably gonna be destroyed in the sanding process. That casual attitude toward something as serious as a serial number on a vintage Gibson would never happen nowadays. Bruce said I should write it on the wall in pencil. "Can't get lost on the wall." So, I walked over to the north side of the back room and wrote it in 1/2 inch numerals. Then, I wrote it down again on a scrap of paper and put it in my pocket. Bruce also carved it into the beat-up back of the guitar in 1/4 inch numerals.

Here's the Provenance Digression of this dark sunburst Gibson Les Paul...

It's the guitar Rick Derringer used on most of both Johnny Winter And albums and about half of the first three Edgar Winter's White Trash albums. Yes, I own the guitar that went dadadadah duda da dahhh da da da duda on the recording of Edgar's "Frankenstein." On page 163 of "The Beauty of the Burst," by Yasuhiko Iwanade, a high-end Japanese coffee-table photo book devoted exclusively to vintage sunburst Les Pauls (true guitar porn), there is a picture of Rick playing this guitar. But, much cooler, in "Beatles' Gear" by Andy Babiuk, there's an amazing story that briefly mentions this dark Les Paul, which I was totally unaware of until I read Andy's book. It turns out that "Lucy," the red Les Paul that George Harrison is using in the promo-film of "Revolution," and his all time favorite guitar, was originally owned by Rick Derringer. In early 1967, Rick had his banged up old gold 1957 Les Paul refinished by Gibson in Kalamazoo the bright wine red of the SG series. But, once refinished, Rick no longer liked the guitar. He took it to Danny Armstrong's shop in New York City. Rick's quote says on page 225, "... I traded the red Les Paul for a sunburst one." A day or two later, Eric Clapton walked into Danny's shop looking for a gift for George Harrison and bought Rick's red Les Paul, who became Lucy. This dark Les Paul was the "sunburst one" that Rick got in that trade. Yes, it's even lightly dusted with Beatles lore.

Fast forward two years to May 2nd, 1972. I had become a semi-permanent fixture at Guitar Lab. I was no longer working there, but dropping by two or three times a week and hanging out, usually after my freshman classes at CCNY (the one year I did of college... 3 A's, 4 B's, 1 Incomplete). Guitar Lab, now in a larger space two blocks uptown, had a small room where the north and south walls each had, at any given time, about 7 or 8 guitars hanging from hooks. On the south wall were guitars in various states of repair, lacquer drying, glue taking, etc.; on the north wall were guitars for sale on consignment.

I walked into Guitar Lab at about 1:30pm that Tuesday and saw, for the first time since that week in July of 1970, Rick Derringer's dark sunburst 1958 Gibson Les Paul on the north wall. I turned to Carl Thompson, and said, "You've got Rick's Les Paul on the wrong wall, Carl." He replied, "No, I don't. Ricky called about a hour ago and told us to sell it. He wants $600 and he owes us $50 for the fret job we just did on it."

Without batting an eye, I said, "Carl, it's sold. Okay! It's sold! Take it down right now! I'll be back with $650 today. Please put it in the back room for me. Just give me a couple of hours. It's SOLD!"

"Okay. Sure, Binky. Take it easy," and he walked over and took it down.

I ran to the elevator. I ran out of that building. I ran to the 20-minute IRT subway ride. I ran to my house in Brooklyn Heights. I ran to my room to get my savings account passbook. I ran to the bank. I ran to the teller. Sweating, chest heaving, I handed her my passbook, and I told her I wanted to close my account. She looked alarmed and said that she'd be right back.

I'd been working two jobs for a year, Wednesdays and Fridays in a small perfume factory, and Saturdays and Sundays at the New York Times as a copyboy. That's another story! I had exactly $652.80 in my account saved from these two small salaries (I still have that little bank book). Money I was saving for a sunburst Les Paul, should one ever turn up, truth be told.

Now, this bank was one of those old cathedrals to money, literally as large as a good- sized church, everything pale tan marble, glass, brass, 35-foot ceiling, everyone speaking in hushed tones. The teller returned with an older man in a dark suit, obviously some very senior presence. He started in with a speech about how impressed he was that a young man my age, a teenager(!), had had the discipline to save this much money and how he really thought "... you should consider what you're about to do and..."

"GIVE ME MY MONEY NOW!" I bellowed at the absolute top of my lungs, the reverberations slamming around that marble cavern. The bank official, beet red, a combination of anger and embarrassment no doubt, turned to the teller and said quietly, "Give him his money." and walked away without looking at me again.

I ran back to the IRT subway. I ran back to Guitar Lab. Got out the largest wad of bills I'd ever had in my pocket and I counted out the 32 twenties and a ten. Carl wrote me a receipt. I thanked him and then got back on the subway to Brooklyn. I got back to my block, and quickly walked to my Tuesday-afternoon-empty home, opened the front door, walked in my living room, opened the guitar case I'd just carried from 49th St. and Broadway, took out the dark Les Paul, held it up to the mirror hanging over the fireplace, and said out loud...

"I am holding this sunburst Les Paul in front of the mirror, in my own living room this time, and... this is my guitar."

I would personally like to thank Ron Middlebrook at Centerstream Publishing for having enough faith in me to publish two versions of BURST BELIEVERS.

Ron, it's a pleasure working with you and I hope we can do something in the future.

I also want to thank everyone who helped in any way, I truly could not have done it without your help.

It was a labor of love for me and I hope everyone who has a passion for Gibson Les Pauls enjoys looking at the photos and reading the stories. I'm very grateful to the players and collectors who made these two editions possible. Keep on rockin', All the best.

Vic DaPra

Index

Guitars

Index

More Great Books from Centerstream...

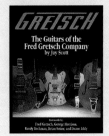

More Great Books from Centerstream...

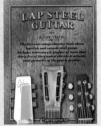

LAP STEEL GUITAR
by Andy Volk

This first-ever comprehensive book about lap-steel and console steel guitars includes: interviews and profiles of more than 35 of the greatest electric and acoustic steel guitarists of the past and present, representing most forms of music played in the world today. Also includes resources for guitars, amplifiers, accessories, instructional materials, steel guitar tunings; and much more.

00000320 336 pages $35.00

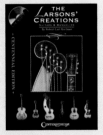

THE LARSONS' CREATIONS – CENTENNIAL EDITION
Guitars & Mandolins
by Robert Carl Hartman

This book is an account of two brothers who were premier producers of stringed instruments in the early part of this century. Swedish immigrant cabinet makers Carl and August Larson made instruments under the brand names of Maurer, Prairie State, Euphonon, W.J. Dyer & Bro., Wm. C. Stahl, and under their own name, and their highly collectible creations are considered today to be some of the finest ever made. This volume includes 16 pages of full-color photos, classic advertisements and catalogs, and a CD featuring guitarist Muriel Anderson playing 11 songs on 11 Larson instruments.

00001043 Hardcover Book/CD Pack $65.00
00001042 Softcover Book/CD Pack $45.00

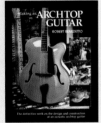

MAKING AN ARCHTOP GUITAR
by Robert Benedetto

The definitive work on the design and construction of an acoustic archtop guitar by one of the most talented luthiers of the twentieth century. Benedetto shows all aspects of construction, even through marketing your finished work. Includes a list of suppliers; a list of serial numbers for Benedetto guitars; full-color plates; photos from the author's personal scrapbook; and fold-out templates.

00000174 260 pages $39.95

MUSIC MAN: 1978 TO 1982 (AND THEN SOME!)
The Other Side of the Story
by Frank W/M Green

Legendary for their construction and longevity, Music Man amps have earned the trust and respect of musicians worldwide. The company was the brainchild of industry vets Leo Fender, Forrest White, and Tom Walker. This book examines the latter – the company's "genius chief pilot/navigator" – particularly during the productive epoch from 1978 to 1982.

00001100 ....$24.95

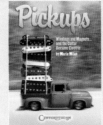

PICKUPS, WINDINGS AND MAGNETS
... And the Guitar Became Electric
by Mario Milan

Guitar collectors rejoice! The first book to examine pickups in detail is here! Covers everything from the first experiments to classic models conceived for Rickenbacker, Gibson, Fender, Gretsch, Danelectro, Epiphone, and others, with an overview of Japanese and European manufacturers. Includes a 32-page color section of the most popular models and rarities, a timeline, info on building pickups and technical specs, and biographical notes on George Beauchamp, Leo Fender, Seth Lover, Larry DiMarzio, and Seymour Duncan.

00001026 ....$29.95

RICKENBACKER
by Richard Smith

A complete and illustrated history of the development of Rickenbacker instruments from 1931 to the present, complete with information and full-color photos of the many Rickenbacker artists.

00000098 256 pages $35.00

WASHBURN PREWAR INSTRUMENT STYLES
Guitars, Mandolins, Banjos and Ukuleles 1883-1940
By Hubert Pleijsier

The vintage guitar collecting market continues to grow. This book is the first of its kind to report on pre-war Washburn guitars, mandolins, banjos and ukuleles. It contains detailed information about more than 450 instrument styles, serial numbering schemes and estimated production totals. A gorgeous 32-page color photo section of the most collectibles will make this book a "must" for players and collectors alike.

00001176 272 pages $45.00

RING THE BANJAR!
The Banjo in America from Folklore to Factory
by Robert Lloyd Webb

This is a second edition of a publication originally published to coincide with an exhibition of the same name at the Massachusetts Institute of Technology Museum. Includes information on the banjo's enduring popularity, the banjo makers of Boston, instruments from the exhibition, a glossary and bibliography of the banjo, and more.

00000087 102 pages $24.95

P.O. Box 17878 - Anaheim Hills, CA 92817

(714) 779-9390   www.centerstream-usa.com

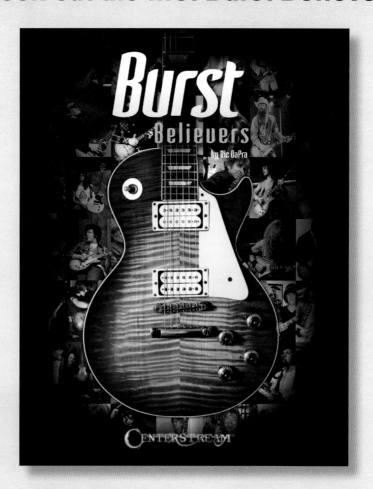